What People A[...]
Bob Hazlett and [...]

Imagine reading a book that will rewire your brain. Instead of negativity and depression, you will function on your God-created level in both your emotions and your daily living. *Think like Heaven* will do that for you if you read its truths and apply them. Bob Hazlett is an amazing, engaging writer and thinker. This book is transparent, challenging, and brilliant. You need to read it. It will change your life!

—*Dr. Cindy Jacobs*
Cofounder, Generals International, Dallas, Texas

Bob Hazlett is an amazing prophetic voice in our day. A tremendous teacher, he has spoken at my Global School of Supernatural Ministry every year since its founding. I am excited to recommend his new book, *Think like Heaven*. It is an important work that challenges us to be willing to renounce our cultural mind-set in light of gaining the mind-set of heaven's culture. Bob helps us to identify blind spots in our thinking and to learn how to perceive reality according to heaven rather than according to the skepticism of earth.

—*Dr. Randy Clark*
Founder and overseer, The Apostolic Network of Global Awakening

It is a marvelous and sublime truth that we are seated in heavenly places, as St. Paul described. Its reality demands that we comprehend what it means to sit in such a realm for the purpose of ruling and ordering the whole of life from that dimension. The old adage that someone is "too heavenly minded to be of any earthly good" isn't valid. In fact, unless we are heavenly minded, as far as the eternal purpose of the Father is concerned, we are of no earthly good in the advance of God's intentions. In *Think like Heaven*, Bob Hazlett has done a *masterful* job of "opening up the heavens" for you as a believer. It's a game changer; and, more important, it's a life changer!

—*Bishop Mark J. Chironna, MA, Ph.D.*
Mark Chironna Ministries
Church on the Living Edge, Orlando, Florida

Bob Hazlett is not just a prophet. He is also a friend of mine and—most important—a friend of God. He has such a clear way of teaching the prophetic. His book *The Roar* blew me away, and I have recommended it to so many people. His second book, *Think like Heaven*, is a masterpiece that will change the way you think about yourself and the world around you. This book brings simplicity to the supernatural. It will transform your mind and help you to become a world transformer. I recommend *Think like Heaven* to everyone who wants to learn like a child and grow into maturity.

—*Todd White*
Evangelist, Lifestyle Christianity

Bob Hazlett is one of the most accurate, humble, and Spirit-led prophets I have ever encountered. *Think like Heaven* will open you up to realms of the renewed mind you never dreamed you could experience. Brace for impact!

—*Robby Dawkins*
Author, pastor, and equipper
robbydawkins.com

Bob Hazlett is not only a dear and trusted friend of mine whom the Lord has used in many ways to bless me and the Vineyard Movement in Germany, Austria, and Switzerland, but he is also a marvelous teacher on the prophetic and on the local church. His book *Think like Heaven* helps people to discover their spiritual potential, no matter how much their past may speak against it. It shows clearly that the Lord loves to use ordinary people for an extraordinary job.

—*Martin Buehlmann*
Leader of the Vineyard Movement in Germany, Austria, and Switzerland
Team leader of the Berlin Vineyard, Germany

In 2010, Bob Hazlett gave me a prophetic word that came straight from heaven. This gave me the courage and conviction to leave the comforts of American success, sell everything I owned, leave family and friends, and embark on the adventure of a lifetime in Africa. Without this strong validation of all that God was telling me, I might have missed out on my destiny. Bob has since spoken numerous times into my life, and it has been critical to have this godly direction as I implement the vision God has given me for lasting economic transformation.

—*Donald Larson*
Founder and CEO, Sunshine Nut Company, Mozambique

I have known Prophet Bob Hazlett for more than seven years. He is a humble man who hears amazing things from the Lord. He has spoken into the lives of multitudes with great accuracy and revelation. Bob says, "Like Jesus, we can identify the sources of our thoughts and confront them with truth." Knowing God's truth will bring transformation that will enable you to see heaven intersect earth. His new book, *Think like Heaven: Change Your Thinking, Change Your World*, will indeed rock your world!

—*Dr. Alan N. Keiran*
Captain, U.S. Navy Chaplain Corps (Ret.)
Cofounder, Dunamis International Ministries
Author, *Take Charge of Your Destiny*

I've known Bob for years, and he really gets it. His ability to take God's Word and spiritual promises and principles and apply them to the real world that we live in every day makes him an invaluable asset to the Christian community and to people in general. *Think like Heaven* is just another example of Bob sharing freely with the rest of us what has been given to him.

—*Jared James*
Jared James Enterprises
Speaker and author, *Get Out of YOUR Way!*

Bob Hazlett's new book, *Think like Heaven*, is a training manual dedicated to transforming our minds so that we can view life through God's eternal perspective and bring hope to this desperate and dying planet. Bob teaches us how to align our thinking with God's heart so that we can walk in our divine mandate as world-changers and history-makers. Every Christian needs to read this book! Without question, it will change your thinking and transform the world around you.

—*Kris Vallotton*
Senior Associate Leader, Bethel Church, Redding, California

Think like Heaven is a key to living from heaven's perspective. It enables readers to go on a journey of learning how to bring heaven's rule down to earth. Not long ago, I lost the companies I had founded and became bankrupt. Over the years that I've known Bob—and especially during that time of loss—he has helped me to learn how to listen to the right voice. He taught me that sometimes we have to pay the price to get to the next level. Yet, by paying that price, or losing something, we've actually already arrived at that next level.

When Bob and I first met, he prophesied specific details about my family and me, which was something that I had never experienced before. He said that we'd be moving from Switzerland to the West, where we now live, in California. We hadn't told anyone of our dream, or our wish list, but Bob knew everything—even the colors inside the home that we would decide to buy. Bob's prophetic words of knowledge helped to restore my vision, and, through seeing it more clearly again, I was reminded of who was really in charge—and He is a much better Savior than I am!

—*Mark Fix*
Prophetic visionary; entrepreneur; private investor; founder and board member of several international companies, including Globacom, Ltd.

LaQuita –
You will release
strength to people
with the joy of
the Lord.

THINK LIKE
HEAVEN

CHANGE YOUR THINKING,
CHANGE YOUR WORLD

THINK LIKE HEAVEN

CHANGE YOUR THINKING, CHANGE YOUR WORLD

BOB HAZLETT

WHITAKER
HOUSE

THINK LIKE HEAVEN:
Change Your Thinking, Change Your World

Bob Hazlett
www.bobhazlett.org
info@bobhazlett.org

ISBN: 978-1-62911-333-3
eBook ISBN: 978-1-62911-334-0
Printed in the United States of America
© 2015 by Bob Hazlett

Whitaker House
1030 Hunt Valley Circle
New Kensington, PA 15068
www.whitakerhouse.com

Library of Congress Cataloging-in-Publication Data

Hazlett, Bob, 1966-
Think like heaven : change your thinking, change your world / Bob Hazlett.
    pages cm
Includes bibliographical references.
  ISBN 978-1-62911-333-3 (trade pbk. : alk. paper) — ISBN 978-1-62911-334-0 (ebook)
1. Christian life. 2. Thought and thinking--Religious aspects—Christianity. I. Title.
BV4501.3.H397 2015
248.4—dc23
                        2015002174

3 4 5 6 7 8 9 10 11 **W** 22 21 20 19 18 17 16

Contents

Foreword by Bill Johnson

Think like Heaven addresses one of my favorite subjects—the renewed mind. As a follower of Jesus, I have committed my life to living in, and exploring, the beauty of Godlike thinking. I said yes to this process well over a decade ago. As a result, I live with an awareness that God works within me daily in this regard. Few things excite me more than the idea of seeing the way God sees and thinking the way He thinks. One of my main ambitions is to "live from heaven," while helping others to think like heaven, also. This really is a central purpose of my life.

The renewed mind is a gift that God has made available to all of us through His grace in Christ. It is not something I can earn, as it has already been given to me. Yet, without cooperation on my part, it remains a seemingly unreachable ideal—something that is in my heavenly "account" but not yet in my possession. Because it requires my cooperation, this quest carries with it the constant reminder that I have so far to go, so much to learn. Such a realization might cause either frustration or hunger to rise within me, depending on the role I allow hope to have in my life. Now, it's impossible to discover the heart of God for us and not be possessed with hope. And so, my heart is full of hope, and I'm very hungry for the *more* that is spoken of in this book.

Think like Heaven came as an answer to my hunger for more of God. But little did I realize how much I was in need of what the author, Bob Hazlett, lives and communicates so well. This book has been a wake-up call for me—a wonderful, grace-filled wake-up call. In reading this manuscript, I have become aware, on a whole new level, of how much I don't know. That sounds painful. Yet my new awareness is the *opposite* of painful. My heart leaps with anticipation of the *more* that God is bringing into my life in this season, spurred on by these pages. I feel summoned by the King of Glory, my heavenly Father, into a journey I've already said yes to. That may sound strange, but it is as accurate a description as I can give. I'm saying yes to God again and again.

Think like Heaven is filled with brilliant insights and powerful expressions from a child of God who has truly yielded to the gracious work of a perfect Father. I recommend this book to every believer, everywhere! In fact, I think it's possible for unbelievers who read this book to become hungry for what they were born for—a personal relationship with the almighty God.

I'm so glad that this book has been written. May God use it in ways we never thought possible and, in the process, enable us to have the impact on our culture that all of heaven is waiting to see unfold.

Bob Hazlett is one of the purest and most trusted prophets I've ever met. His ministry is so encouraging and life-giving. I am always impressed with what he has to say—both because of his insights and because of his ability to hear the voice of God. I commend to you the man and his book, *Think like Heaven*.

—*Bill Johnson*
Senior Leader, Bethel Church, Redding, California
Author, *The Supernatural Power of a Transformed Mind* and
Hosting the Presence

Foreword by Lance Wallnau

I work with writers, and some of them are best-selling authors. I rank Bob up there with them, for two reasons. First, he does not repeat what other people have already said—his thinking is original! Even though he is addressing subject matter you might think you know, he finds a way to give you a different perspective. The result is that he makes his subjects fresh, vital, and invigorating. His mind is like Jacob's ladder: It brings you up one step at a time into a heavenly perspective so that you can come down one step at a time into a potentially new spiritual walk. You will enjoy all that this gifted man has to say, not only in this book but in other works yet to come.

—*Lance Wallnau*
Founder, Lance Learning Group

Introduction: Heavenly Minded = Earthly Amazing!

 Bob Hazlett @bob_hazlett
The most radical thing you can do today is to
believe what God says about you, and then live like
it is true! #ThinklikeHeaven

Writing a book is a daunting task. Attempting to use black letters on a white page to transport people to a world of living color can be intimidating. With every writing project I undertake, my appreciation for books and authors increases!

Recently, I purchased a collector's set of the first novels I read in my teen years: C. S. Lewis' Space Trilogy. Lewis was arguably the most colorful writer of the twentieth century, definitely more famous for his fairy tales than for his Sci-Fi/Fantasy books. As a teen, however, I was drawn more to planetary travel than to fauns and princesses, so the trilogy hit my literary sweet spot.

Lewis was a masterful storyteller, but, more than that, he knew where stories came from, explaining, "All my seven Narnia books, and my three science-fiction books, began with seeing pictures in my head. At first they were not a story, just pictures."[1]

You could say that pictures are what stories are made of.

Your Life Is Your "Story"

Let's apply that concept to your life. Your life is *your* story, and it began with a picture. God pictured you before the foundation of the world. You read that exactly right: God saw you before there *was* a world. That is a radical statement, by any stretch of the imagination, but it's true.

I am a student of God's Word, as well as a teacher of the Word. I am also a lifelong learner of God's ways of speaking in the here and now. To understand how He speaks, it helps to know how He has spoken in the past. The first time God's voice was heard on the earth, all of creation responded. The unseen became seen, and the uncreated was created. Everything we see—and much that we cannot see—came from words spoken by God. Jesus, who is "the Word become flesh" (see John 1:14), revealed the origin of God's creation words when He said, *"The mouth speaks what the heart is full of"* (Luke 6:45).

So, what was God's heart full of before He created the earth? The answer is found in Ephesians 1:4: *"He chose us* [called us out, spoke about us[2]] *in him before the creation of the world…."* Even before there were the heavens and the earth, God's heart was full of thoughts and words about us! The heavens and the earth were created with you and me in mind.

God's thoughts produced words, and His words produced what He envisioned. To see life through God's lens is to think like heaven. It involves "seeing" more than what we can physically see, taste, touch, hear, or smell. This is a dimension of life that we pay too little attention to. Life lived solely through our earthly experiences and environments is incomplete. It leaves us half empty, with a black-and-white view of ourselves and of the world around us.

There is much more living than that ahead for you—but you first have to *see* it. When you know where your story comes from, you will know where you are going. You will see the *amazing* picture God sees…and you will see it in living color.

Gridiron Dreams

Every child has a dream. More important, every child is a dreamer. I was a big one! In my heart and mind, I was a football player. My passion was obvious: I collected football cards; I had football curtains on my bedroom window; my wardrobe screamed football. I ate, drank, and slept the game. As far as I was concerned, every level surface, from the schoolyard to the street to the yard at the side of our house, was a potential football field.

Nothing got between me and football. Having started school a year early, I was academically accelerated but physically smaller than most of my classmates. On the field, the apparent minus became a plus. I was radically over-motivated and routinely underestimated. What I lacked in physical stature, I made up for in passion.

In my last year of junior high, I showed up for team tryouts. My friend David was the only guy who was smaller than I was. The coach looked at the two of us with that "here come our new water boys" expression.

His assumption was understandable. Tryouts amounted to a single game, appropriately named "Kill the Kid with the Ball." Game Plan A was simple: Get the ball and keep it by whatever means necessary. If that failed, Game Plan B was equally simple: Catch the guy who beat you to the ball, make him cough it up, and take it to the end zone—by whatever means necessary.

Those were the only rules. Obviously, the coach wasn't looking for the most talented players; he was looking for the ones with the most heart. He had plenty of candidates to choose from. Some of the guys were so big, they looked like high school kids who'd been held back as many times as they had been promoted. I'm pretty sure one kid named Arnold could have grown a full beard at the age of twelve.

From the start of tryouts, the competition was fierce. The first ball kicked was captured by one of the biggest players. His glory was short-lived. Bearded or not, Arnold was bigger than the kid with the ball. The run ended when Arnold slammed him to the ground.

A pileup ensued, and I saw an opportunity to use my size to my advantage. Diving into the heap and making my way to the bottom, I pried the ball from the big kid's hands. It helped that Arnold had softened my target. But the bearded wonder's size worked against him. Before he knew it, I'd used my stature, high-level pain tolerance, and quick legs to own the play. In no time, the ball and I reached the end zone, and my passion won me a first-string spot on the Pasack Colts, the first undefeated and unscored-against team in the history of the school district.

Playing for the Colts earned me the only sports trophy I ever won. I display it proudly to this day. Although I never got the position I really wanted, my competitive, no-holds-barred attitude put me in the right-guard slot. I played next to Arnold, the first-string right tackle.

Making the top squad in junior-high football set my expectations for high school. Being up against bigger and stronger opponents didn't faze me. I wanted to play with the big boys and had learned how to beat them. So, when I arrived at high-school tryouts, I was confident. About one hundred other players showed up, too, but that did not bother me. I believed my junior-high experience was about to repeat itself.

While I waited for my name to be called, I heard two upperclassmen jawing. One was the highly respected quarterback from my former championship team. "Look at all these small freshmen," he said. "They think they'll make the team, but they don't have a chance."

His words shook my thinking. They altered how I saw myself. They changed what I dreamed of doing. They changed my actions, too. I walked out of those tryouts and never played competitive football again.

Life didn't exactly become an ash heap when my football dreams fizzled. I found a great after-school job at a restaurant and became the youngest night manager they ever had. My boss mentored me and entrusted me with a lot of responsibility. I was expected to lead a team, close up shop at the end of the day, and make nightly bank deposits. For becoming part of a national promotion team for the franchise, I was awarded a scholarship.

I had no deep sense of remorse about quitting football—but I did regret letting another person's opinion shape my thinking. Like any kid, dreaming big had always come easily to me. That changed when I started hanging around older and larger kids whose thinking got smaller as they grew bigger.

No wonder Jesus said we have to become like children to enter the kingdom of God! (See Matthew 18:3; Mark 10:15; Luke 18:17.) If we will continue to dream big, He will confound the "wise" through our "foolishness." (See 1 Corinthians 1:27.) God welcomes our big dreams, whatever our age. He knows big dreamers will change old ways of thinking into His ways of *thinking like heaven*.

A Rough Start

The shaking of my athletic confidence in high school was hard for me, but it wasn't earth-shattering. Many young people suffer far worse setbacks than that every day. Some never seem to regain their footing; others somehow manage to become world-changers.

One we might include in the second group was apparently born with the deck stacked against him—King David. Not much is known about David's early years, before the prophet Samuel arrived at the house of David's father, Jesse, to anoint one of Jesse's sons as the next king of Israel. Yet David made some statements in his psalms that might point to a difficult childhood. For example, he wrote, *"Even my own brothers pretend they don't know me; they treat me like a stranger....I am the favorite topic of town gossip, and all the drunks sing about me"* (Psalm 69:8, 12 NLT), and *"I was brought forth in iniquity, and in sin my mother conceived me"* (Psalm 51:5 NASB).

These statements do not necessarily refer to David's childhood, but there is a story in Jewish lore that David's father, Jesse, shunned him, falsely believing he was the result of an illicit affair. If the story from Jewish tradition is accurate—and let's suppose it is for the purpose of our discussion—the treatment would have caused David emotional trauma. (We at least know that Jesse did not even acknowledge the existence of David when the prophet Samuel first asked to see his sons.) Rejection would have been stamped on David's psyche. His soul would have absorbed years of lies and accusations.[3]

David was Jesse's flesh and blood, a rightful member of the family. Yet, as the runt of the litter and an outcast, David was sent with the family's flocks into dangerous terrain. As tradition has it, his accusers supposed,

"With any luck, he'll be mauled by a lion, or maybe a bear." When he returned from the fields in one piece, they banned him from eating dinner with the family. David's banishment from the dinner table was a metaphor for his emotional exile.[4] God's handpicked king would have some hurdles to jump.

From the Garden of Eden to a Garden Tomb

David's experience of isolation and rejection ultimately had its origin in the garden of Eden, where sin debuted. In the blink of an eye, after sinning, human beings were separated from their Maker. Their spirits went dark. Their physical immortality was lost. Their mental and emotional states suffered. The blow to their soul was massive. The only class of created being that had been made in God's image and likeness (see Genesis 1:26–27) now bore an image scarred by sin.

Emotional pain became a fact of human existence. It stirred the compartments of the soul, where our thoughts, desires, and feelings are headquartered. Life—which had once worked so perfectly—became very complicated after the fall of humanity. The garden-dwellers were banished from Eden to live as fallen people in a fallen world, in which their minds played tricks on them, their wills proved fragile, and their emotions ran circles around them.

Like any human being, David lived with the fallout of Adam and Eve's blunder. His family history was the product of it. Those who should have loved him the most, hurt him the worst. The emotional hit was direct, like a grenade to the heart.

But there is more to David's story. Alone with his father's sheep, David found his roots—in heaven. In his isolation, he cultivated his inner life. He excelled as a musician, seer, and poet. Day in and day out, the shepherd boy worshipped the Lover of his soul and even glimpsed his coming Messiah. David's troubles remained, but they paled in comparison to what he saw and experienced in God's presence. The boy banned from the family table was invited by God Himself to eat at a heavenly one. (See Psalm 23:5.) The "fatherless" child would become, in essence, father to a nation. When the Messiah whom he glimpsed rode a donkey into Jerusalem, people shouted,

*"'Hosanna!' 'Blessed is he who comes in the name of the Lord!' 'Blessed is the coming kingdom **of our father David!**'"* (Mark 11:9–10).

David's turnaround may have been stellar, but the coming of Messiah reverberated through the cosmos. Jesus, the One of whom David prophesied, came to earth as promised and overturned the serpent's dark works. Even as His body lay in a garden tomb, the garden fall was coming undone. When the Savior's work was complete, invisible realms were opened to mankind. The Savior invited His redeemed to sit with Him in heavenly places. (See Ephesians 2:6.)

Live from the Next Level

Even as king, David suffered his share of heartaches. Every human being does. Most of us kissed off at least one dream before we reached adulthood. Some dreams get written off the way mine did. We think we are being "practical," but we are dabbling in self-doubt. Other dreams stay around longer but taunt us like carrots dangling from sticks. They seem to hang just far enough out of reach to remain perpetually unfulfilled.

Both issues are common in life. The second one masquerades as the sense that we are getting ready for the "next level," but we never arrive there. In reality, I believe God is making us aware that He has already opened the next level to us. He's not only getting us ready, but He's also getting something ready for us. When we realize that we are already "there," spiritually, we can live *from* the next level instead of *toward* it.

That is an important theme of this book. It's not a self-help concept or something I say to make people feel better about themselves. It is a prophetic reality based on kingdom truth. It's about an eternal mind-set and an understanding of our spiritual position in Christ. The apostle Paul described this concept in his letter to the church at Colossae:

> *Since, then, you have been raised with Christ, set your hearts on things above, where Christ is, seated at the right hand of God. Set your minds on things above, not on earthly things. For you died, and your life is now hidden with Christ in God.*   (Colossians 3:1–3)

Paul said that we are to think *from* where we are, which is *"raised with Christ...seated at the right hand of God."* We are already there—with Him and in Him. Knowing this is so important, because our tendency is to see everything from an earthbound view. God warned us about that a long time ago:

> *"For my thoughts are not your thoughts, neither are your ways my ways,"* declares the LORD. *"As the heavens are higher than the earth, so are my ways higher than your ways and my thoughts than your thoughts."*   (Isaiah 55:8–9)

The heavens are higher than the earth, but we are seated in heavenly places. It is not that we are *going* to be there; we are there *already*. How frustrating and self-limiting it would be (and is) *not* to realize our position and to continue to think *toward* it. Yet how completely amazing and productive life is when we think *from* the position we already hold!

Here's how amazing it is: God's thoughts and ways are higher, so His words are, too. In the same chapter of Isaiah, He said His Word soaks the earth and makes it flourish: *"It will not return to me empty, but will accomplish what I desire and achieve the purpose for which I sent it"* (Isaiah 55:11).

Thoughts are like seeds, words are like water; put them together, and they produce something that is fruitful! God is telling us that when it comes to our thinking, higher is better. It can literally change the world.

It's in There

Thinking like heaven not only means knowing where we are but also being aware of what we already have. There are things God put in us long ago that we have not yet noticed. He will manifest them externally at the right time, but we don't have to be oblivious to them in the meantime.

When I was still in school and living at home, my parents took in young adults who became part of our family. Two young Cuban men stayed with us for about three years. They happened to arrive during my first week of Spanish language class at school, so I was appointed chief interpreter—despite the fact that I could not yet speak a lick of Spanish. My skill set improved over the course of three years, because I spent a lot of time with our Cuban friends. I ended up learning the language, including some words I had no business knowing.

Eventually, I forgot the bad words, but I never lost my love for the Latino culture, community, and language. For some reason, God's purposes in this experience escaped me, but the connection kept showing up. Years later, I was ordained into the prophetic ministry while in South America. I have been there dozens of times now. Yet, even after three years of immersion in the language, five years of studying Spanish in school, and many trips to Latin America, I rarely spoke the language.

Recently, while I was waiting for my ride at an airport, a man whom I did not know approached me, holding out his cell phone and speaking a language I did not understand. Thinking he wanted me to do something with his phone, I reached for it. Just then, my phone rang, and I took the call. The man kept talking to me, and I realized that he was speaking Spanish. Being reasonably good at handling one conversation at a time, I politely said, "Un momento."

I continued my phone conversation and hoped someone would come along and help the Spanish-speaking man. Solving my own problems in English seemed to be enough of a challenge at the time. How in the world would I solve a stranger's problem on *his* phone, in *his* language?

God saw the situation differently and had something in mind. When my call ended, the man started talking to me again, and I actually understood what he was saying. He had just flown in from Santo Domingo and was expecting his daughter to pick him up. He needed to call her, but his phone worked only in Santo Domingo. He wanted to give me her number so I could call her and tell her where to meet him.

Now things were getting exciting! Not only did I understand the man, but I dialed his daughter and gave her all the details in Spanish. Next thing I knew, I got a word of knowledge for him. So I gave him the word in Spanish and prayed for him in Spanish, and he got healed—not at an altar in an English-speaking church but at an airport where the language barrier came down!

Then it dawned on me: What God had put inside me twenty years earlier was everything I needed that day. I never saw it coming, and I hadn't planned for it. But He had prepared me. The seed had been in place all that time, and now it had germinated. My only job was to become aware of it and to let God shine through me.

There are things inside you that will arise out of dormancy when you least expect it—and at just the right time.

Know Heaven; Think Heaven

Thinking *like* heaven starts with thinking *about* heaven. The Bible is a great place to begin, because it is filled with pictures of heaven. I love thinking about them and envisioning the scenes. I imagine the twenty-four elders falling prostrate before God and laying their crowns before His throne. I see the seraphim and can almost hear the rumble as they shout, "*'Holy, holy, holy is the Lord God Almighty,' who was, and is, and is to come*" (Revelation 4:8).

Heaven is amazing, but not amazing enough to contain the One who made it. He did not create heaven as His living quarters or as a place for our disembodied spirits to go after death. God created us to be immortal, not to "die and go to heaven." He created heaven so He could interact with us through it. It is an environment ordained for communication with the living.

Theologian Meredith G. Kline wrote about the "two-register cosmos" and the "biblical drama, which features constant interaction between the upper and lower registers."[5] The interaction in the biblical drama is the ongoing conversation between the very relational, omnipresent God and His people.

Meredith Kline also said that Genesis 1:1 affirms God's creation of the two registers, one of which is "the invisible realm of the divine Glory and angelic beings."[6] The apostle Paul explained Genesis 1:1 by "declaring that the Son created 'all things that are in heaven and that are in earth, visible and invisible, whether they be thrones, or dominions, or principalities, or powers' (Col. 1:16; cf. John 1:1–3)."[7] Christ created heaven and earth and everything in them.

The enormity of God and His creation is mind-boggling. God gives us a sense of the scale: "*Heaven is my throne, and the earth is my footstool*" (Isaiah 66:1). That is a picture of a very big God. It helps explain how His view of heaven differs from our ideas about where He lives. Another, more ordinary, picture explains what I mean. It is a *very* earthly analogy, so a disclaimer is in order: It is meant as a learning aid, not a reflection on God.

With that settled, consider the everyday "man chair." Do you have a picture in your mind? Can you see a recliner (perhaps the chair that a loved one claims as the command post from which he monitors Sunday football and carries on an occasional conversation)?

Now suppose I visited a new friend's house to watch a game. It would not take long for me to figure out which chair was his, even if he were nowhere in sight. His wife would confirm my suspicions with that pained look that says, "Yup, that's it. The one with the salsa stains."

As lived-in as the chair might be, my friend does not actually *live* in it. The chair is his "throne"—the "sacred" place from which he "rules." From his recliner, he visits with folks like me, watches the news, and interacts with his family. When his kids want to sit on Daddy's lap, they go to his chair and climb on up.

Likewise, heaven is God's throne. He created it to serve a purpose similar to that of my friend's chair. It is the place where God interacts with His "kids." Heaven is not just "up there" somewhere. It is an atmosphere, a plane on which God exists and through which He and His own communicate together. Before the fall of humanity, this communication was unbroken. The fall created a breach, but Jesus has redeemed us and restored our access to God. Heaven is here, because His presence is here with us. At the same time, we are seated with Him in heavenly places.

You cannot see heaven with your physical eyes, but it is a real place. More than being the destination where you go after you die, it is the place where you came from. You cannot go to heaven without first having come from heaven (see John 3:13), in which case you can go there to climb up on Daddy's lap anytime. And when the day comes that you are absent from your body, you will be present with your Lord (see 2 Corinthians 5:8 NKJV, KJV), seeing heaven in all its beauty.

Hebrews 12:22–23 paints the following picture of heaven, the angels, and God's family:

> *You have come to Mount Zion, to the city of the living God, the heavenly Jerusalem. You have come to thousands upon thousands of angels in joyful assembly, to the church of the firstborn, whose names are written in heaven. You have come to God, the Judge of all, to the spirits of the righteous made perfect....*

Heaven is not where God "lives." He cannot be contained. He desires to commune with us, so He created an atmosphere in which we could meet. That atmosphere is called *heaven*.

When God wanted to interact with man, in the flesh, He sent Jesus. *"For in Christ all the fullness of the Deity lives in bodily form"* (Colossians 2:9). The fullness of God was in Jesus in bodily form. In a similar manner, God put the fullness of who He is into a realm He calls heaven. The apostle Paul visited heaven, and he gave us a glimpse of what he saw: *"Praise be to the God and Father of our Lord Jesus Christ, who has blessed us in the heavenly realms with every spiritual blessing in Christ"* (Ephesians 1:3). Every blessing that is in Christ is available for us in heaven.

It's in the Cloud

Jesus carried the essence of God in bodily form, and heaven embodies the essence of God in spiritual form. Throughout the Bible, the physical picture of heaven is often a cloud. Heaven hovered over the earth at Creation, visited with and guided Moses in the wilderness, and conversed with Jesus on the top of a mountain. In each instance, whoever or whatever entered the cloud was changed, and what was in the cloud changed the world around them.

Are you struggling with the idea of a "virtual" world that exists but is unseen? One that contains stored-up resources and information and has the power to interact on an individual and global scale alike, regardless of time or space? It's easy to understand—look no further than your laptop or cell phone. All that we do and say, all of our history and future plans, all of our resources and health records, are stored in a "virtual, computerized" cloud. It's interesting that the name we use for storing large amounts of digital data is the same as that of the picture God chose to show us what He has available for us. It is as if God has been getting us ready for the reality of heaven on earth, inviting us to access heaven and be changed by it. God provided what you need in order to be transformed and to transform the world around you: It's in the cloud!

Being from Heaven

There is something about knowing where you came from that stays with you. For example, in regard to the town or city in which you grew up, you might have since relocated to another part of the nation or even taken a trip to the moon. Or, you might have started life in a poor neighborhood and subsequently become a billionaire living in a mansion. But the place where you came from will always be a part of you.

When the Pharisee Nicodemus sought out Jesus, he walked the razor's edge of controversy. The sect in which he held a high position believed that Jesus was a blasphemer. For him to meet with Jesus was politically dangerous. Nicodemus therefore came to Him in the dark of night. Still, he risked his reputation. His reason for doing so is revealed in what he said to Jesus: *"Rabbi, we know that you are a teacher who has come from God"* (John 3:2).

Jesus' answer to Nicodemus turned the Pharisee's world inside out. He said, in essence, "To tell you the truth, unless you are born again, you have no clue where I came from." (See John 3:3–21.)

All Nicodemus heard was the impossibility of what Jesus seemed to be saying. Bound by earthly thinking, the man envisioned bizarre child-birthing scenarios that had nothing to do with reality or anything Jesus was saying. Nicodemus could not grasp Jesus' real point, which was about being born from above—born from heaven. The idea did not fit the Pharisee's worldview. He was not born from heaven, so he could not go there, even in his mind.

If you are born again, you are born from above. Understanding the implications of that fact radically affects the way you live. When you know where you come from, you live confident of what is yours. You know where you already are and what you already have.

That is what it means to think like heaven. Again, you are not "getting ready" for the next level; you are there now. Let me paraphrase Paul's words from his letter to the Colossians that I shared earlier: "You have been raised with Christ. You are from heaven, so think like it." (See Colossians 3:1–3.)

Heaven's Generation

As emotionally damaged as David was in his youth, he learned to think like a man rooted in heaven. Worship took him there. Shut out by loved ones and left to fellowship with the flocks, David sang love songs to his Maker. He poured out his heart and entered prophetic realms in which he saw Messiah's reign, centuries before Christ came. David then prophesied to generations yet to be born—generations that would be born again.

Imagine David as a born-again man indwelt by the Holy Spirit. Not only would he have boldly defeated lions, bears, and uncircumcised Philistines, but he also would have rejoiced in the redemption he'd been able to merely glimpse in the invisible realm. Now imagine yourself that way, not because I asked you to, but because *that is who you are.*

This book was written for a generation of Davids who desire to think like heaven in spite of—and even because of—life's struggles. It was also written for the modern-day Daniels who converse with both heaven and earth, speak the world's languages and understand its concerns, draw from heaven's provision, and offer heaven's solutions. (See, for example, Daniel 1.) Because they understand what God shows them (revelation), they are able to generate a new culture—the culture of God's eternal kingdom.

The generation I dream of talks to billionaires and babies, adversaries and angels, virtually in the same breath. They sing great hymns and prophesy in hip-hop. They know the world's lingo, but they follow God's ways. They love people and relate to them wherever they are and however they look. They do it whether they are loved in return or ridiculed for what they believe.

For these heaven-thinkers, all things are possible.

Notes

1. P. H. Brazier, *C. S. Lewis—On the Christ of a Religious Economy, 3.1: 1. Creation and Sub-creation* [C. S. Lewis: Revelation and the Christ series] (Eugene, OR: Pickwick Publications, 2013), 133.
2. The Greek word translated *"chosen"* in Ephesians 1:4 is *eklegō*. This term is a combination of two words: *ek*, meaning "out from," and *lego*, meaning "to relate in words." The implication is "to choose by calling out through the spoken word."
3. See Chana Weisberg, "Nitzevet, Mother of David," TheJewishWoman.org, http://www.chabad.org/theJewishWoman/article_cdo/aid/280331/jewish/Nitzevet-Mother-of-David.htm.
4. Ibid.
5. Meredith G. Kline, "Space and Time in the Genesis Cosmogony," from *Perspectives on Science and Christian Faith* 48:2–15 (1996), The American Scientific Affiliation, http://www.asa3.org/ASA/PSCF/1996/PSCF3-96Kline.html.
6. Ibid.
7. Ibid.

1

What Are You Thinking?

Have you ever imagined being alive when Jesus walked the earth? I think most Christ followers have. The next thought that usually pops up involves the people who mocked Him. We like to believe that we never would have done such a thing. We wonder, *What were they thinking?*

To say that the reactions to Jesus' earthly ministry were mixed would be an understatement. Even as people flocked to Him, naysayers rose against Him. It happened in Capernaum. People came in droves. The crowd grew so large that a man desperate for healing could find only one way to Jesus—down through the roof.

The four friends who carried the man on a mat made an opening in the structure and lowered him through it, mat and all. Imagine the thoughts running through people's minds as the ceiling gave way and debris showered the scene! Can you hear the shouts? "What are those morons doing? Can't they see the Man is preaching?"

Jesus saw the interruption differently. He did not gripe about it; He was moved by it. "*When Jesus saw their faith, he said to the paralyzed man, 'Son, your sins are forgiven'*" (Mark 2:5).

Other witnesses of this event were moved, too, but not necessarily in the same way Jesus was. "*Some teachers of the law were sitting there, thinking to themselves, 'Why does this fellow talk like that? He's blaspheming! Who can forgive sins but God alone?'*" (Mark 2:6–7).

The naysayers were in the moment, but they missed the point. They mistrusted Jesus' intent because they misunderstood who He was. Their mental filters did not signal the arrival of Messiah but the presence of an "enemy" in the camp. They did not treat Him badly because He had it coming but because they *thought* He did. They thought the paralyzed man had it coming, too. Infirmity was seen as divine payback for the sin of a person or his family. If you were blind, lame, or infirm in any other way, you deserved it. So, when Jesus healed the man, these naysayers saw it as a sure sign that He was not from God.

As angered as this group was by Jesus' words, they managed to keep their lips sealed. They stewed in silence, probably expecting their resentment to go unnoticed. It didn't. "*Immediately Jesus knew in his spirit that this was what they were thinking in their hearts, and he said to them, 'Why are you thinking these things?'*" (Mark 2:8).

Jesus saw right through them. But *how?*

"Heaven-Think"

Jesus came from heaven to earth to change people's hearts and to take people's infirmities—including that of the paralyzed man—upon Himself. (See Isaiah 53:4–5.)

To Jesus, the man's bizarre entrance was not an opportunity to complain or to reprimand but to do what He had come to do. He did not react to the falling debris or to the diseased thinking of the Pharisees. His response made room for the thinking of eyewitnesses to be transformed. The crowd marveled and praised God.

It takes just one person who thinks like heaven to neutralize "earth-think" and to change the culture.

Perception by the Spirit

Jesus, as God in the flesh, retained His divine nature but laid aside His divine attributes. He perceived people's thoughts by relying on the Holy Spirit, who empowered Him. So, when the teachers of the law judged Jesus, He "read their mail."

It got their attention. (It usually does!) Jesus wasn't showing off or trying to embarrass anyone. He was fulfilling the Father's purposes. Jesus' own words reveal the seamlessness of His connection with His Father: *"Very truly I tell you, the Son can do nothing by himself; he can do only what he sees his Father doing, because whatever the Father does the Son also does"* (John 5:19).

Jesus was sent *"to seek and to save the lost"* (Luke 19:10). The religious leaders thought they had religion all buttoned down. They did, but it wasn't the kind of religion God had in mind. So, Jesus responded prophetically to their accusations. He spoke in order to awaken them from the deep sleep of their distorted mind-sets. Tradition and misperception had them so bound that they could not discern God's heart. Even after centuries of waiting for Messiah, they did not realize that He had arrived.

Distorted thinking is like a virus that sickens the host and also spreads to others. As it infects people, it makes lies and even bloodlust palatable to them. There is no shortage of examples in history. In the twentieth century, the perverse thinking of one man, Adolf Hitler, infected the masses until millions became tolerant of perverse ideas, and then of outright genocide. The Cambodian "revolutionary" Pol Pot was similarly lethal. Two million Cambodians are believed to have perished in less than four years under his brutal rule.

Jesus showed how thinking like heaven has the opposite effect of distorted thinking. He confronted people with truth—the only antidote to infected mind-sets. He did it regardless of their social standing or the political consequences. Pharisees, teachers of the law, fishermen, and friends all got a dose. When the Pharisee Nicodemus had it dispensed to him, his paradigms imploded. (See John 3.) When Jesus called hypocrites *"whitewashed tombs,"* their deadened hearts were exposed. (See Matthew 23:27.) When Martha was confronted by *"the resurrection and the life,"* new spiritual realms were revealed to her. (See John 11:1–44.)

Jesus did all things in love. But living in love does not mean validating everybody's ideas. Jesus did not tolerate self-serving, distracting, or devilish thoughts. *He confronted them with truth.* He held Himself to a high standard—thinking, saying, and doing only what His Father thought, said, and did. He conveyed this standard to His followers, while understanding their human weaknesses. His aim was to deliver them from bondage, and the process had to start with their thinking.

You've Got Mail

Has anyone ever "read your mail"? How did your experience compare or contrast with the account from Mark 2:1–12?

Invisible but Real

Spiritual things are not as ethereal as some might think. In fact, they have substance. Faith is a perfect example. Hebrews says, *"Faith is the substance of things hoped for, the evidence of things not seen"* (Hebrews 11:1 NKJV, KJV). That is a heavenly statement! Faith cannot be seen; it is not like something that can be stored on a pantry shelf. Yet *faith is substance.* In other words, it is real.

This truth is paradoxical to the natural mind. We expect real things to be visible. Yet the whole of creation was made from that which was invisible. The writer of Hebrews hinted that our natural minds would wrestle with this concept. He said, *"**By faith** we understand that the universe was formed at God's command, so that what is seen was not made out of what was visible"* (Hebrews 11:3). The apostle Paul also talked about visible and invisible things:

> *The Son is the image of the invisible God, the firstborn over all creation. For in him all things were created: things in heaven and on earth, visible and invisible, whether thrones or powers or rulers or authorities; all things have been created through him and for him.*
>
> (Colossians 1:15–16)

God is invisible—but, in Jesus, He became visible for a season. Today, we cannot see God with our natural, physical eyes. God's throne, as well as the organization of Satan's kingdom, is also invisible to us. Yet they are real. So is time. We cannot see time or hold it in our hands, but we see its effects, such as when we observe the growth of a baby from infancy to childhood to adolescence to adulthood; or, when we notice the gradual appearance of wrinkles on our bodies in places we never thought they would develop.

Thoughts are real, too. Like time, they are intangible but produce tangible results. If you have ever regretted saying something hurtful to a loved one, you know how real and lasting the effects of your words can be. Thinking is also catalytic; it ignites chain reactions. Thoughts become words…words become actions…actions become reality. If you think about something long enough, you will eventually vocalize it. If you keep saying it, you will act on it; and if you act on it long enough, you will *become* it.

Thoughts impact people individually, but they also create and transform groups. Individuals coalesce around ideas. Cultures are formed wherever like-minded people gather. You cannot physically see the underlying *groupthink*, but you can see the culture that develops from it. If excellence is a company's hallmark, you can trace it back to the group's shared mind-set. If a nation is known for protecting individual freedoms, it is because that ideal is engrained in its thinking.

Thoughts are real, and thoughts transform.

Thoughts Come from Somewhere

Have you ever awakened to a thought that seemed to have come out of nowhere? I have. One morning, my waking thoughts were so strong, they seemed almost audible. "Who are you?" a voice snarled. "You don't even have a job description. *You are a loser!*"

Talk about a "wake-up call"!

At the time, I was on staff at a church and also doing itinerant ministry. In retrospect, I can see that God was transitioning me into my current assignment and settling some identity issues. I had been questioning my role and asking Him, "Am I a pastor? Am I an evangelist? Am I a prophet? And what *is* prophetic ministry, anyway?"

Clarifying my role was a priority for me. Identifying the voice I'd heard was important, too. At first, not knowing what to pray, I prayed in the Spirit. Praying in a spiritual language is praying the language of heaven. The apostle Paul said that this Spirit-talk allows us to speak *"mysteries"*—not from our own thinking but by the Holy Spirit. (See 1 Corinthians 14:2.) We pray what we don't understand so that we can understand what God wants to do. I would rather pray words that I can't explain than pray what I shouldn't.

The Language of Heaven

The Bible says that spiritual language is available to all believers through the power of the Holy Spirit. Some people say you can have the Holy Spirit without the Spirit-talk. My response is, "If it's available, I want it!" If the Bible said I could slam-dunk a basketball by the power of the Holy Spirit, I'd want that, too. Why not?

I love basketball, but spiritual language is much better than hoops. No offense, Michael Jordan.

Soon after I prayed in the Spirit, God answered with the truth I needed. A Scripture popped into my mind that I hadn't even known I had memorized. It was 1 John 3:8: *"The reason the Son of God appeared was to destroy the devil's work."* Heavenly illumination lit my earthly lightbulb: "That's your title: You are My son. Your assignment is to destroy the devil's works. That's your job description." James 1:21 says to *"receive with meekness the implanted word, which is able to save your souls"* (NKJV). God had planted the verse from 1 John so deep within me that I didn't consciously remember it, but when my soul was in turmoil, heaven brought it to the surface.

Wow! In an instant, God had addressed the same identity vacuum that the accusing voice had seized upon earlier that morning. I did not realize until later that another "access point" had been opened in my life when the church board members had discussed my job description among themselves at a meeting the night before. They had not spent the evening accusing me. They had simply been addressing issues important to the church. Yet their discussion had created an opening in the atmosphere that the "accuser of the brethren" (see Revelation 12:10 NKJV, KJV) had been happy to exploit.

As rude an awakening as I experienced that day, it was also providential. Only hours later, my senior leader called me into his office and said, "Bob, you were the topic of our board meeting last night. The board has no job description for you. They don't know if you're a pastor or an evangelist. They want me to find out."

Whoa, I thought. *God totally prepared me for something I had no idea was coming.*

I answered my boss without hesitation. "That's easy. I can write out my job description for you right now."

"Really?" he asked, a little surprised.

"Yeah, no problem."

My Father had already given me the answer, so I wrote it down on a sheet of paper and slid it across the table. It was short and sweet: "Title: Son of God. Job description: Destroy the works of the devil." This opened up a larger conversation and gave us both a clear sense of direction. When we were done, my official job description was in black and white.

I learned several things that day. First, every thought comes from somewhere, and sometimes it comes from a combination of places. To handle thoughts accurately, you have to identify their sources. Generally, they come from four places:

+ the atmosphere
+ the accuser
+ adversity
+ heaven

Let's take a look at each of these sources.

Thoughts from the Atmosphere

Have you ever left a store and taken a song home with you? While you're picking out a ripe melon, a catchy tune plays overhead. The music is designed to change the atmosphere and induce you to spend more money. Whether or not you are consciously aware of what is happening, the song stays with you. Hours later, the melon is long gone, but you are still humming the tune.

Unsolicited thoughts are "hitchhikers" that hang out in the atmosphere. If you let them, they'll climb into your head and stay until you show them the door.

Thoughts from the Accuser

The "accuser of the brethren" is the devil. Scripture says he accuses us before God day and night. (See Revelation 12:10.) When the words *You are a loser!* rang out in my mind, it was the accuser speaking. My wife wasn't talking in her sleep, thank God. The board members weren't taking potshots at me, either. And, although the thoughts entered my mind, they were not *my* thoughts. They were lies designed to slander me and to debase me.

If you accept demonic accusations, they can become fixtures in your thinking. But if you identify their source, you will realize that they don't belong to you, and you will reject them as the lies they are.

Thoughts from Adversity

Adversity can affect your long-term thinking in powerful ways, as well. Imagine that you were bitten by a dog as a child. You can see how dog-related fears might become part of your outlook. Even if you grew to be six foot something and could bench-press a couple hundred pounds, the sudden move of a Teacup Chihuahua might raise your heart rate. The reaction would be based on an adverse experience that had imprinted your psyche and now causes you to see new experiences through old filters.

Thoughts developed in adversity don't automatically leave when the adverse experience is over. They have to be recognized, held up to the light, and escorted to the trash heap.

Thoughts from Heaven

Heaven's thinking is what we are after. Scripture tells us to live from every word proceeding from God's mouth. (See Deuteronomy 8:3; Matthew 4:4.) That is exactly what Jesus did. He listened for what His Father was saying and then spoke and acted accordingly. Jesus was not insulated from thoughts that challenged His purpose, yet He mastered them. He filtered out "hitchhikers" in the atmosphere. He rejected the devil's suggestions in the wilderness. He kept negative experiences with powerful people in perspective. And, He refused to allow any fear of His impending crucifixion to paralyze Him.

As Jesus did, we can identify the sources of our thoughts and confront them with truth. We *can* live in the midst of the world's chaos without being ruled by it. The answer is to create what I call *the atmosphere of our arising*. It is the atmosphere David understood so well—the realm of praise that healed his emotional wounds and prepared him to fulfill God's massive plan for his life.

David said to God, *"You are holy, enthroned in the praises of Israel"* (Psalm 22:3 NKJV). The word translated *"praises"* here comes from a unique root word for praise, *halal*, which means "to be (clamorously) foolish" and "to make a show."[1] David did not care who was watching him or what anyone thought as he danced before the ark of the covenant. (See 1 Chronicles

15:28–29; 2 Samuel 6:16–22.) The ark had been designated as the seat of God's presence in the tabernacle and temple.

Through worship, David created an atmosphere in which God's throne became "Daddy's chair." Meeting with his Father again and again in this intimate place transformed his soul. The repeatedly rejected "runt of the litter" became the fierce defender of Israel who took down Goliath with a slingshot and a stone. (See 1 Samuel 17.)

Opposing Cultures

The term *culture war* is popular these days. Whether or not we believe such a thing exists, we can agree that two very different cultures are facing off in our world: the culture of heaven and the culture of hell.

The "war" is not new. These two kingdoms have opposed each other from before the beginning of time. They are pictured in a couple of well-known Bible accounts. The first story is that of the Tower of Babel. At this time in history, the whole world was united by a common language, and people were moving eastward looking for a place to settle down. (See Genesis 11:1–2.) They said, *"Come, let us build ourselves a city, with a tower that reaches to the heavens, so that we may make a name for ourselves; otherwise we will be scattered over the face of the whole earth"* (Genesis 11:4).

That plan was at odds with God's purposes. After the flood, God had blessed Noah and his sons and told them to *"fill the earth"* (Genesis 9:1). There was plenty of territory to cover, but the tower-builders wanted to stay local and make a name for themselves. Their thinking was hellish; their tower was an attempt to overcome heaven. The idea was futile. Reaching from earth to heaven was impossible. The real genius would have been to build in the opposite direction—*from heaven to earth*. That was essentially what Jesus offered Nicodemus: to be born from above and to start building from there. (See John 3.)

The second biblical story reveals the culture of heaven. Jesus gave His disciples a pop quiz, and one disciple came up with the right answer.

[Jesus] *asked his disciples, "Who do people say the Son of Man is?" They replied, "Some say John the Baptist; others say Elijah; and still others, Jeremiah or one of the prophets." "But what about you?" he asked. "Who do you say I am?" Simon Peter answered, "You are the Messiah, the Son of the living God." Jesus replied, "Blessed are you, Simon son of Jonah, for this was not revealed to you by flesh and blood, but by my Father in heaven."* (Matthew 16:13–17)

Peter answered Jesus' question from the Father's perspective. The disciple known for putting his foot in his mouth aced the oral exam! Jesus gave Peter the spiritual equivalent of a high five and explained the importance of his revelation to the world:

I tell you that you are Peter, and on this rock I will build my church, and the gates of Hades will not overcome it. I will give you the keys of the kingdom of heaven; whatever you bind on earth will be bound in heaven, and whatever you loose on earth will be loosed in heaven. (Matthew 16:18–19)

In other words: "Good job, Peter! You didn't get this idea from the world. You got it from heaven. If enough people learn to think this way, they will bring heaven's environment to earth and decimate the culture of hell."

Imagine how Peter felt. While his comrades had fished for an answer, he had heard straight from heaven and said something that was light-years beyond his natural thinking. Based on Peter's personality, I'm guessing he felt like the big man on campus. Instead of a dunce cap, he got himself a gold star.

Of course, Jesus would not have banished anyone to the corner, but Peter might have pictured himself ending up there. As passionate as he was, he did not always think like Christ. Right after his earthshaking revelation, he slipped right back into "Peter-think." It happened when Jesus said that He would soon die and be resurrected. Peter took exception to this idea and advised Jesus against the plan. Suddenly, the disciple who'd had heavenly insight into the Son was at odds with the Son's primary mission.

Peter took [Jesus] aside and began to rebuke him. "Never, Lord!" he said. "This shall never happen to you!" Jesus turned and said to Peter,

"Get behind me, Satan! You are a stumbling block to me; you do not have in mind the concerns of God, but merely human concerns."

(Matthew 16:22–23)

Ouch. Peter got to wear the pointy hat after all. In a single conversation, he went from star student to cleaning the chalkboards. Jesus' statement *"Get behind me, Satan!"* warns *us* to discern the sources of *our* thoughts. It is also a powerful reminder not to allow the thinking of others to draw us away from our heavenly mission. Jesus was neither impressed by Peter's first statement nor intimidated by his second. He was focused on heaven. In the long run (and in all seriousness), Peter was transformed and was powerfully used to establish the culture of heaven on earth. His revelation stands in stark contrast to the mind-set of the tower-builders in Genesis. They were self-promoting and self-serving. Peter ultimately devoted his life to glorifying and serving his King, and he was martyred.

I have witnessed this kind of transformation in others and have experienced it in my own thinking. Several years ago, after a particularly powerful meeting, a woman approached me and asked if I would address her church group. The topic, as I understood it, was the power of the Spirit, so I agreed.

When I received the formal invitation, I discovered that we were not talking about the same spirit. The words *church* and *Christian* were conspicuously absent. I did an Internet search on the group and realized that I had booked myself to speak at an "interfaith, New-Age church."

Knowing that my thinking about Jesus would be different from theirs, I asked Him what He thought about the invitation. The answer came quickly, as if Jesus had said, "I don't know what you're doing, but I'm going!"

My thinking was immediately transformed. Jesus is not afraid to hang out with people who don't believe in Him, even if they are antagonistic toward Him. I realized that I should see it the same way He does. Since that day, I have addressed many people and groups who are from other faiths or have no faith at all. Jesus is seriously *not* offended by folks who find Him offensive!

The meeting with the New Age group proved to be powerful. Outwardly, it was nonconfrontational. I told them who Jesus is to me—the unique Son of God who died and rose again. I told them about my best friend, the Holy Spirit, and I prayed for the sick in Jesus' name. Among the people who were healed was a woman with severe nerve and disk damage. The healing was so dramatic that it got the attention of the group's leaders. As the meeting wrapped up, they stood around me with their arms folded and said, "We don't believe Jesus is who you say He is, but that woman was not healed in a crystal healing meeting two weeks ago or in the energy healing meeting last week. But Jesus' name healed her."

They believed crystals and energy could heal, but neither had helped the woman. "Please come back," they said, "and show us how you did that in Jesus' name."

I asked Jesus about it, and He said, "Yep!"

So, we went back *five times in one year*! The group advertised the second meeting in the newspaper and among alternative healing circles. Attendance was double that of the first meeting and included close to one hundred alternative healing practitioners. None of them believed in Jesus, but they soon would!

I told them that Jesus came to heal body, soul, and spirit, and I demonstrated the first two. Powerful physical healings occurred, and some people received emotional freedom. When I explained the uniqueness of Jesus and how His resurrection provided spiritual healing, about one-fourth of the people asked Jesus to bring this healing into their lives. (One of the Greek words translated as "save" or "saved" in the New Testament is *sozo*. It means "to heal, preserve, save"[2] and "to rescue from danger or destruction."[3])

It was an amazing moment, although one of the leaders didn't think so—the one who had originally invited me. When she approached me after the meeting, her posture was defensive, and her face looked very serious. "I like you and the power you bring, but I am not on the same page with you about Jesus. I do not believe He is the Son of God."

Already forming in my mind and on my lips were these words from Jesus' conversation with Nicodemus: "Unless you are born again, you cannot see the kingdom." (See John 3:3.) But heaven hijacked my words.

Instead, Jesus' conversation with Peter came to mind: "My Father in heaven revealed this to you." (See Matthew 16:17.) In other words, if you want to see heaven, you need heaven's help.

Then I heard myself say, "Just like Jesus' disciples followed Him as healer, teacher, and prophet, you follow Him that way. One day, the Father will reveal to you who Jesus is, and the lightbulb will go on. When that happens, call me."

I was clear about who Jesus is, but she didn't need my faith—she needed God to give her faith in His Son. Two months later, she called. The lightbulb had turned on, and Jesus had become for her more than a healer, a teacher, or a prophet. In her words, He had become her Savior!

Hunger for the Supernatural

Have you observed how preoccupied with vampires many people have been in the last few years? Have you noticed a similar zombie craze? People can't seem to get enough of otherworldly stuff—but why?

I believe these obsessions reveal cultural deficits. People crave the supernatural and are crying out for something that reaches beyond the visible realm. They want to believe in life after death. Deep down, they know there is more to life than what they see. They are correct, and we can point them in the right direction—toward heaven.

The Benefits of "Losing It"

When Peter offered his two cents about the Lord's imminent death, Jesus dismantled the hellish idea and gave the disciples this truth:

Whoever wants to be my disciple must deny themselves and take up their cross and follow me. For whoever wants to save their life will lose it, but whoever loses their life for me will find it.

(Matthew 16:24–25)

Jesus was not suggesting suicide as a form of worship. The word translated *"life"* in this passage is the Greek word *psuche*, or *psychē*, which refers to the soul[4] (composed of the mind, the will, and the emotions). Jesus' point was simple: "If you try to preserve your old way of thinking, dreaming, and feeling, you will lose it. But if you are willing to lose it, you will find something far better than you imagined."

The transformation of our way of thinking is a process that Jesus is ready to undertake with us. You saw His surgical strike on Nicodemus's belief system. After freaking him out with the words *"born again,"* Jesus upset his understanding of the curse (the result of the fall of humanity). For Jews, Messiah was the "anti-curse." Jesus turned that idea on its head, telling Nicodemus, *"Just as Moses lifted up the snake in the wilderness, so the Son of Man must be lifted up, that everyone who believes may have eternal life in him"* (John 3:14–15).

Can you imagine the rate at which Nicodemus's synapses were fried? "Wait, I thought the serpent was cursed. The Messiah is supposed to remove the curse, not become it!"

Not everything Nicodemus believed was flat wrong, but his paradigm was aging out. Christ's arrival created a new reality that this Pharisee's belief system could not contain. Jesus knew the man had to break out of his religious boundaries and accept the Savior's mission, or die under the curse. So Jesus rattled his cage some more.

Nicodemus was transformed. Just how much of the change happened during that one conversation, I can't say. But the man who had been afraid to meet with Jesus in daylight later made a public revelation of his relationship with Him. When Jesus' body was removed from the cross, Nicodemus joined Joseph of Arimathea in giving Him a proper burial. Nicodemus brought seventy-five pounds of myrrh and aloes, and the two men wrapped the body themselves. (See John 19:38–42.)

Jesus taught Nicodemus how to think like heaven. He does the same for us. If we are willing to lose our natural thinking, we will gain heaven's point of view and live as He planned for us to live—"*from glory to glory*" (2 Corinthians 3:18).

Thinking like Heaven

1. In Mark 2, why did the teachers of the law mistake Jesus for an enemy? What do you think made their perspective so rigid? Can "good ideas" conflict with heaven's ideas? If so, how?

2. Imagine yourself in a conversation with someone who lives (however sincerely) according to an idea that is untrue. How can you speak to that person in love without validating ideas that conflict with God's?

3. Spiritually speaking, what (if anything) about invisible things regularly challenges your faith? Explain. Has your view changed since reading this chapter? If so, how?

4. What evidence do you see in your immediate environment of hell's culture? Of heaven's culture? Do you believe that heaven will prevail? How might you be part of the solution?

5. Draw up a "lose-it" list of mind-sets that limit your ability to live "*from glory to glory.*" What do you think has held these mind-sets in place till now?

Notes

1. Biblesoft's New Exhaustive Strong's Numbers and Concordance with Expanded Greek-Hebrew Dictionary, CD-ROM, Biblesoft, Inc. and International Bible Translators, Inc. (1994, 2003, 2006), s.v. "tehillah" (OT 8416); "halal" (OT 1984).
2. Ibid., s.v. "sozo" (NT 4982).
3. Blue Letter Bible, Greek Lexicon, 1996–2014, s.v. "sozo" (Strong's NT 4982), https://www.blueletterbible.org/lang/lexicon/lexicon.cfm?Strongs=G4982&t=KJV.
4. Ibid., s.v. "psychē" (Strong's NT 5590), https://www.blueletterbible.org/lang/lexicon/lexicon.cfm?Strongs=G5590&t=KJV.

2

Arise in Your Thinking

 Bob Hazlet @bob_hazlett
Heaven was not intended as a "retirement home" for deceased believers but as a place from which real life is lived. Adam was created to never die. So, heaven was created so that human beings could interact with a living God! #ThinklikeHeaven

↩   ⇄   ★   •••

Location, location, location. From the ground, the smallest hill can limit your line of sight. But if you are perched high above the earth, even the Rockies are no obstacle. When we rise above the natural landscape, it causes things to shift within us. Life's angles look different. Our perspective is changed. Likewise, when we arise in our spiritual thinking, our outlook is transformed, so that God's purposes may be fulfilled and His glory may be seen.

> *Arise, shine, for your light has come, and the glory of the* Lord *rises upon you. See, darkness covers the earth and thick darkness is over the peoples, but the* Lord *rises upon you and his glory appears over you.*
> (Isaiah 60:1–2)

"Arise, shine…." God is specific: First you arise, and then you shine. Arising snaps the tether of earthbound thinking. I see this often in

prophetic ministry. There is nothing better than seeing the moment when someone arises and shines!

Recently, I met a young woman and saw the word *scholarship* above her head. God was showing me her struggle. He revealed it so that He could deliver her. The answer she needed was already prepared, but she did not yet perceive it. Her mind was so tightly wrapped around the problem that she could not see the solution.

I told her what God had told me: "You have been thinking that you can't finish school because you have no money. But if you ask for a scholarship, you will get it."

Her eyes widened. She said she had downloaded some scholarship applications the week before but had not completed them because she believed the answer would be "No." Her assumption had paralyzed her. Where opportunity awaited, she saw only deficit. It was just a mind-set, but it was jamming her destiny. Until her thinking arose, she would stay stuck. So, God sent a prophetic word that revealed His heart and crushed the lie of impossibility.

That is what heavenly thinking does. In two increments, a prophetic word releases what God has in mind:

1. It realigns human thought with God's intent, equipping an individual to proclaim His will. The person delivering the prophetic word is also realigned to release the right ministry. (An accurate word given from the wrong perspective can have the wrong results.)

2. It issues permission for something already in mind *or* something unexpected. For the young woman who needed a scholarship, a prophetic word affirmed her educational desires and confirmed God's intended provision. Her changed perspective *permitted* her to pursue His plan for her life.

The Art of Arising

Let's look again at Isaiah 60:1–2:

Arise, shine, for your light has come, and the glory of the Lord rises upon you. See, darkness covers the earth and thick darkness is over the peoples, but the LORD *rises upon you and his glory appears over you.*

Notice that the first two words are verbs—one active and one reflexive, or passive. *Arise* is an intentional act, but *shine* is not. You don't decide to shine; however, when you arise, God's light shines through you. Additionally, the Hebrew words translated *"arise"* and *"rises"* are distinct. The first one literally means "to stand up."[1] The second gives the idea of emanation and means "to shoot forth beams."[2] Again: You stand up, and God shines through you. You make your move, and God makes His!

Do you remember the story about the Spanish-speaking man at the airport? My doubts about being able to help him were natural. What God had in mind was something *super*natural. When I got over my doubts enough to act on what I knew, God gave me access to what I did not know. That is when the floodgates of healing opened and God fulfilled His larger purpose.

If I had stalled until I thought my skill set was perfect, the encounter would have ended as a "nothingburger." Someone else would have called the man's daughter, and the man would have left the airport in the same condition in which I had found him. That could easily have happened. I am *really* glad it didn't.

Recall what Paul said in Colossians 3:1–2: *"Since, then, you have been raised with Christ, set your hearts on things above, where Christ is, seated at the right hand of God. Set your minds on things above, not on earthly things."* Speaking to born-again people, he said we should set our minds on the place where we came from.

In verse 2, the Greek word translated *"minds"* is *phroneo,* which refers to a mental disposition.[3] So, our way of seeing things should arise to the level of our position with Christ. That is our vantage point. This is spiritual but also logical: How can we see and respond like lowlanders when we are seated on high?

Arise and Shine 101

1. You act on what you know (your part).

2. God will provide what you don't know (His grace).

3. God will be enthroned in the situation and glorified through it.

The Atmosphere of Peace

Earlier, I mentioned *the atmosphere of our arising* in relation to King David's life of praise. This was David's place of solace and restoration, but also of power. In his praises, God was enthroned, and David's life was directed up and out of the depths.

The atmosphere of our arising is an atmosphere of peace—heaven's kind of peace. The world sees peace as the absence of conflict. This is a passive idea that leaves people at the mercy of their environments. That is not God's intent. Peace is not passive but active. In fact, peace is God's government!

> *For to us a child is born, to us a son is given, and the government will be on his shoulders. And he will be called Wonderful Counselor, Mighty God, Everlasting Father, Prince of Peace. Of the greatness of his government and peace there will be no end.* (Isaiah 9:6–7)

Let peace govern your thinking! Let it be your impenetrable shield. Even when warfare surrounds you on all sides, it cannot get past your shield. God's kingdom and government saturate the atmosphere of peace and neutralize the enemy's power. The apostle Paul told the faithful at Rome, "*The God of peace will soon crush Satan under your feet*" (Romans 16:20).

Jesus said, "*The thief comes only to steal and kill and destroy; I have come that they may have life, and have it to the full*" (John 10:10). And, after Jesus distinguished His intent from Satan's, He made the following statements: "*I am the good shepherd…[who] lays down his life for the sheep*" (John 10:11);

"I know my sheep and my sheep know me" (John 10:14); *"My sheep listen to my voice; I know them, and they follow me"* (John 10:27).

Jesus used the metaphor of a shepherd and his sheep because people in an agrarian society could relate to it. They knew that when sheep were grazed outside the city, several shepherds would gather their flocks into a single pen for the night. The next day, each shepherd would call his sheep by name. Because each animal recognized only one voice, it was not distracted by other sounds. The shepherds therefore left with only their own flock.

There are many competing sounds in modern society, but heaven's sound is peace. To hear it, we need to tune out the chatter. It is not easy! I'm as easily distracted as the next guy. In 1997, I almost let some "old noise" steal my future. It happened right after I had experienced the wonders of the Pensacola Revival. A certain prophetic minister was coming to our town, and a pastor friend told me, "Bob, you've got to come and hear this guy."

Two distractions clogged my thinking. I told Pastor Ed about both of them. First, I didn't think I could handle another powerful church service after the intensity of Pensacola. Second, I told him, "I don't believe in prophets."

My wife saw the situation more clearly than I did. She discerned the sound of peace and urged me to change my mind. Like a good sheep, I listened and attended the service—but I took my skepticism with me. Near the end of the meeting, the prophet called me up and said, "You're a pastor, aren't you?"

Well, yeah, I thought, *I'm sitting next to Pastor Ed, so you probably could have figured **that** out.*

Then the prophet "read my mail" and described what was ahead. He laid it all out with such precision that I thought, *If there really are modern-day prophets, this guy might be one.*

God used a prophet to cut through my chatter and to release the sound of peace. When I returned to that church the next day, I learned about forthcoming things that are playing out in my life even now. The man prophesied over my wife, Kimberly, and me, and told me, "You're going to be doing exactly what I'm doing."

That was news! Then he asked me, "Do you know how to break in a new mule?"

"Uh, no."

"You hook the new mule up to an old one," he said, in his thick Arkansas accent.

"OK…" I said, fishing for his point.

"You're the new mule," he said. "You're going to follow me around, and you're going to hear what I hear."

So, I followed him around every night for two weeks, *and I never heard a thing.*

The experience remained a mystery to me until a pastor friend asked me to speak at a youth service. When that night came, something broke wide open. God spoke to me in a way He never had before, by giving me a word of knowledge for a young woman attending the service. He said, "Her boyfriend just broke up with her. Voices are telling her she's worthless and should take her own life."

*What is **that**?* I wondered.

It was the first sign that the prophet's word to me was being fulfilled. He had said I would do what he did and hear what he heard. It was happening! God revealed the woman's situation to me, just as He had revealed my situation to the prophet.

As weighty as these events were, there was a humorous twist to them that God probably chuckled over. Starting that night, for two years, I heard God's voice through a new filter—the Arkansas accent of the prophet. It was a funny way of hearing, but it was heaven's sound, just the same.

Four Roads to Arising

Living our everyday lives and arising in our thinking go hand in hand. Four general areas of our thought lives cover virtually everything we think about:

- How we think about God
- How we think about ourselves
- How we think about life
- How we think about heaven

Again, over the years, our thoughts often get filtered through our experiences, so that our ability to think like heaven is compromised. Let's take a good look at these four areas in relation to thinking like heaven, remembering a Scripture passage we read earlier:

> "For my thoughts are not your thoughts, neither are your ways my ways," declares the LORD. "As the heavens are higher than the earth, so are my ways higher than your ways and my thoughts than your thoughts." (Isaiah 55:8–9)

1. Thinking Differently About God

How we perceive God sets the foundation for how we see ourselves and our world. Whenever He takes us to a new level, He reveals something about Himself that we did not previously know. The first coming of Christ revealed new things. People witnessed Jesus' acts—and marveled. More important, Jesus revealed the invisible God to humanity.

The spirit of wisdom and revelation does the same thing:

> I keep asking that the God of our Lord Jesus Christ, the glorious Father, may give you the Spirit of wisdom and revelation, **so that you may know him better.** I pray that the eyes of your heart may be enlightened in order that you may know the hope to which he has called you.... (Ephesians 1:17–18)

When you know God, He can tell you what is on His heart. If I give you a prophetic word about what God wants to do in your life, I also need to reveal *Him*. Otherwise, you will get only part of the meaning without fully understanding the hope to which you are called. Knowing the *who* is more important than knowing the *what*.

Some key aspects about God will help us to arise in our thinking about Him.

He is a relational God. Anyone who has ever walked with God has been invited to take new "territory" and to think differently about Him. Abraham came from a family of idol-worshippers, but when God spoke to him, his thinking changed. He became fiercely monotheistic; he was deeply committed to the one true and living God. Instead of honoring dead statues and fetishes, Abraham became the friend of the relational God who makes covenants with people.

He is a God who lives with us. Centuries later, Moses discovered that God is not only relational but also "habitational." Moses and the Israelites lived and traveled with God; He appeared in their midst as a pillar of cloud by day and a pillar of fire by night. (See, for example, Exodus 13:21–22.) It spoiled Moses for anything else. Even after God promised to stay with him, Moses pressed the issue, saying, *"If your Presence does not go with us, do not send us up from here"* (Exodus 33:15).

He is a God who is our Father. When Jesus came, He revealed still another aspect of God: His fatherhood. The idea wrecked the Jewish mindset and particularly offended religious leaders. The controversy reached a boiling point when Jewish leaders plotted Jesus' murder for His alleged blasphemy. (See John 5:17–18.)

He is a personal God. Two thousand years after Christ, these historic revelations remain intact. We interact with a relational God who is also habitational, and we embrace Him as our Father. But our understanding of God continues to unfold. In the past twenty or thirty years, He has especially revealed Himself as a personal God—just as He revealed Himself in that way to an Egyptian slave named Hagar, who told Him, *"You are the God who sees me"* (Genesis 16:13); to a tax collector named Zacchaeus, who welcomed Jesus when the Lord singled him out, saying, *"Zacchaeus, come down immediately. I must stay at your house today"* (Luke 19:5); and to many others whom we read about in the Bible. Today, instead of singing *about* God in our worship, we sing *to* Him. We also talk about God as our Husband. (See Isaiah 54:5.)

For men, that idea takes some adjusting to! I remember the first book I read about the Lover of my soul, and the Song of Solomon teachings I heard about twenty years ago. My wife asked me, "What do you think about it?"

"It's like reading a foreign language," I said. I was serious; an understanding of God as my Husband and Lover messed with my "man filters."

To think differently about God means to arise to new territories in Him. To identify any filters that need to come down or to discover gaps in our perception of God, we can ask ourselves two simple questions:

+ What new things does God want me to learn about Him?

+ How do these new things relate to the taking of new spiritual territory?

Be Aware of the Opposition

You have probably heard the expression "New level, new devil." This is not literally accurate; there are no new devils. But you will encounter increasing opposition from Satan when you aggressively step into new spiritual territory and become more intimate with God. The enemy knows that the new things you learn about God will thwart his dark kingdom.

2. Thinking Differently About Yourself

God does not see us according to our shortcomings and past mistakes. He sees us according to the blood of Jesus. That is our real identity, the one we need to see, too. When we arise and see ourselves the way God sees us, He shines through us in the way He desires. This is the new creation reality that Paul wanted us to grasp when he wrote the following:

> Christ's love compels us, because we are convinced that one died for all, and therefore all died. And he died for all, that those who live should no longer live for themselves but for him who died for them and was raised again. (2 Corinthians 5:14–15)

Paul was talking about being "out of our minds"—and in the mind of Christ. When we grasp the weight of Jesus' sacrifice on our behalf, His love becomes real to us. We cannot help but live differently and see ourselves in a new way. If "*all died*," then we are "dead people." Yet we are more alive than ever, because we have also been "*raised with Christ*" (Colossians 3:1). This is how God sees us!

To see ourselves His way is to arise. The truth is that we have *already* arisen with Him. Whether or not we are living that way, it is our assigned station. God calls us to live *from* our arisen place. That is why Paul said, "*We regard no one* [including ourselves] *from a worldly point of view. Though we once regarded Christ in this way, we do so no longer*" (2 Corinthians 5:16).

My thinking about *me* must continually change. When I arise in my thinking, my problems look smaller, and I recognize that my weaknesses can have eternal value if I submit them to God. Instead of being shameful, they allow His strength to be "*made perfect*" in them. (See 2 Corinthians 12:9.) God is not pointing out my flaws to show me how deficient I am. Instead, He is revealing all that He wants to make available to me. He is saying, in effect, "Here is what I want to show you about Myself. Behold Me, and you will reflect Me in this area of your life."

Not too long ago, God showed me something I needed to see in the area of self-control. The issue sprang from my strongly developed sense of justice. Justice is a good thing, but seeing past that grid was hard for me. I received an offensive voice mail message, and my sense of justice took over. The smart thing would have been to delete the message as I would a nasty e-mail. But hearing an actual voice got the better of me, and hitting the redial button seemed like a very good idea. If nothing else, it would have *felt* good to unload on the guy. So, I placed the call. It rang and rang and went to voice mail. I hung up without saying a word.

Frustrated with myself for hanging up, I redialed the number but hit the *end* button even before voice mail kicked in. I dialed the number a third time and did exactly the same thing! It became obvious to me that God had something to do with this, so I went back to my room and spilled my guts to Him.

"All right, God," I said. "I'm going to give You one more chance. Here's exactly what I want to say to this guy, and I know how good it will feel to say it. It won't feel as good later on, but I'll just repent and apologize. Now give me a reason *not* to make the call."

Instead of laying into me, He said, "I don't want to give you a reason. I want to give you My desire."

I was not expecting that answer. Still, the idea had potential, and I thought that, with a tweak, it could be brilliant. All God had to do was remove my desire altogether, and the issue would be solved.

God wasn't buying my idea, so I said, "Show me Your way in the Bible."

He answered, "Jesus in the garden of Gethsemane."

"*What?*"

"Jesus said, 'If it be Your will, let this cup pass from Me.' In other words, going to the cross, becoming sin, and being forsaken by Me was not My Son's will. He didn't want to take on every sickness or become cursed. Then He said, 'Nevertheless, not My will, but Yours, be done.'" (See Matthew 26:39; Luke 22:42.)

The message was loud and clear: Jesus had needed to choose, and I would need to choose, too. So, I lifted my will up to God and chose His will instead of mine. In that instant, the desire to make the phone call evaporated. The whole encounter with God lasted about five minutes. The lesson will last a lifetime. He taught me how to live from His point of view. And He showed me how to think differently about myself.

3. Thinking Differently About Life

God created us to co-labor and cocreate with Him, not through self-effort and striving but by entering the superabundant flow that is His modus operandi. Earlier, we saw a hint of this in John 10:10. Now let's look again at the second half of the verse: "*I have come that they may have life, and that they may have it **more abundantly**"* (NKJV).

The Greek word translated "*more abundantly*" is a strong word. It conveys the sense of a "violently excessive"[4] life, as though God were imposing His magnificence on us. It reminds me of Matthew's statement that "*the kingdom of heaven suffers violence, and the violent take it by force"* (Matthew 11:12 NKJV). This is not ugly, earthly violence but a heavenly kingdom surge. God is extravagant toward us. His generosity is part of the rest that He calls us to enter into—not a passive, kick-back-in-the-recliner rest, but the active rest seen in the exodus of the Israelites from Egypt and in their inheritance of the Promised Land. God took care of His people's every need, but they had to engage in the journey. When He sent manna for them to eat, they had to gather it. When He promised to give them Jericho, they had to march around the city a total of thirteen times, blow the ram's horn, and shout. Their efforts were important but were not enough to knock down the wall. God's grace was the difference-maker. That is what the rest was about, and it produced violently excessive results.

That grace was evident as Jesus hung on the cross. He said few words as He fought for every breath. All physical strength drained from His body, along with His blood. He was dehydrated and should have been delirious. But until His heart stopped beating, He remained actively engaged. Every word He spoke, even as He suffocated, resounded prophetically in the earth and accomplished God's purpose.

Even when we reach our weakest point, we can remain actively engaged in what God is doing in us and through us. We need to draw upon the words and dreams He has given us and share them with whomever He sends our way. God is big enough; He has provided more than what is needed for the task at hand. He has wired us to engage in this violently excessive, superabundant life.

4. Thinking Differently About Heaven

I believe this is a season in which God wants us to understand heaven. Again, we know that heaven was not intended as a "retirement home" for deceased believers. Human beings were never supposed to die but to live forever. Heaven is a place of communion between God and us. It is His throne, His "easy chair," and He invites us to climb up on it to be with Him. When we do, He hands us the "remote control" and says, "Go ahead. Hit *play.* I'm watching the movie of your future. It looks great. Stay and watch it with Me."

God is enthroned in the praises of His people. (See Psalm 22:3 NKJV.) Praise lifts us up into Daddy's chair, where our perspective is transformed. It is an arisen perspective, an ascended way of thinking, that reflects His higher ways and higher thoughts. The beautiful thing is that we have uninterrupted access to it. His invitation is open-ended.

"As it is written: 'Eye has not seen, nor ear heard, nor have entered into the heart of man the things which God has prepared for those who love Him'" (1 Corinthians 2:9 NKJV). When we arise in our thinking, the invisible things will become visible, and Jesus will say, *"Blessed are your eyes because they see, and your ears because they hear"* (Matthew 13:16).

Bringing the Incomparable to the Fallen

The peaceful and powerful culture of heaven is incomparable. The brokenness of the world makes us long for it. Yet, there is another way—an arisen way—of seeing the distinction between the culture of heaven and the culture of hell than merely witnessing the world's brokenness. We can see it through the following example. When Jesus healed the paralyzed man, and the Pharisees' blood boiled, Jesus addressed them directly. His "job description" was to destroy the works of the devil, including hellish thoughts. So, He exposed their thinking and challenged them with truth. (See Mark 2:1–12.) The contrast in cultures was an opportunity for Jesus to bring heaven to earth.

Ever since the fall of humanity in the garden of Eden, the earth has carried a balance sheet of deficits—spiritual, moral, physical, and so forth. When we encounter these deficits, we are tempted to throw our hands up and walk away. But that is not God's will for us or for the world. The cultural deficits we see in people—such as obsessions with sex, witchcraft, or money—are spiritual 9-1-1 calls. The world is sending up distress flares. In essence, their obsessions *prophesy* the aspect of heaven that God wants to bring to earth.

There is no shortage of such deficits. Everyday conversations about gender orientation, the nature of marriage, and the inherent value of life reveal the limitations in some people's thinking. We cannot fix these issues by natural means. If we try, we will only feel defeated. Instead, as Christ's body, we can arise in our thinking and see the opportunities as God does. From His eternal vantage point, hell's culture is *already* defeated!

The world is hungry to know the Almighty. People long for the omnipotent, omnipresent God. Their words betray their desire. The New Agers say, "God is everywhere and in everything." Other people talk about "acts of God." They do not have their facts right; but, instead of shutting them down, we can open the truth and share God's goodness by giving our testimonies. We can say, "God is my Father. Christ lives within me. In Him, I live and move and have my being." (See Acts 17:28.)

The culture of heaven *will* prevail, and we are part of God's plan. As we arise in our thinking, we become a people willing to surrender the deficits in our own souls so we can bring God's soul to our depraved culture.

Thinking like Heaven

1. Have you received a prophetic word in which God has given you permission to do something? Put that "something" into words and ask God to reveal more of His plan.

2. Have you ever opted out of a divine appointment because of earthly chatter? Ask God to reveal specifics about how your awareness of heaven's sound can produce His desired outcomes in your life.

3. When I heard God speaking with the accent of the prophet from Arkansas, it actually helped me to get over my sense of God as an angry father. What false impressions of God have skewed your understanding of Him? Ask Him to show you who He really is.

4. Describe what the term *violently excessive abundance* brings to your mind. Has God given you insight into where this kind of abundance awaits you? Ask Him about it, and ask Him about His purposes in it.

5. Describe a cultural deficit that ruffles your feathers. What adjustments to your perspective might be needed? How is God asking you to reveal Him to others?

Notes

1. Biblesoft's New Exhaustive Strong's Numbers and Concordance, s.v. "quwm" (OT 6965).
2. Ibid., s.v. "rarach" (OT 2224).
3. Ibid., s.v. "phroneo" (NT 5426).
4. Ibid., s.v. "perissos" (NT 4053).

3

No More Fig Leaves

Bob Hazlett @bob_hazlett
A clear conscience gives you confidence. Live like you have no skeletons, no hidden agendas, and no enemy too big for God. It's true! #ThinklikeHeaven #NoMoreFigLeaves

↩ ⇄ ★ •••

Picture the biggest, "baddest" roller coaster in the world. You have to strain to see its highest peaks, but you can hear its riders screaming from half a mile away. How the cars stay on the rails as they plunge, careen, and whip around impossible turns is anyone's guess. The experience is enough to turn your clothing inside out…and to turn your insides outside, too.

For some people, just picturing a roller-coaster ride causes them terror. For others, the bone-jarring trip is a dream come true. I'm in the latter category. I love everything about roller coasters, except waiting in line to ride them again. The jolts and g-forces get my motor going. When the thrill is over, all I want is more.

I remember once riding a fierce roller coaster with my brother. We bought our tickets, buckled in, screamed like crazy, and lived to tell the tale. We took the same ride but had very different experiences. I jumped out of the car and raced back in line. My brother walked away and said, "Never again."

He wasn't the only one who'd had enough. And I wasn't the only one who couldn't get enough. You could say it was a tale of two mountains: "Fear Mountain" and "Fun Mountain." The people in the first group were not wimps. Taking even one whack at the ride required gumption. The people in the second group—well, let's just say they were different. The point is that what each group believed about the roller-coaster experience determined what they did next.

Fear Mountain, Fun Mountain

There were no roller coasters in Moses' day, but at one point during the exodus, he asked the Israelites to line up for the ride of their lives. God had just reminded Moses of how He had decimated Egypt and how He saw Israel as His *"treasured possession"* (Exodus 19:5). Then He told Moses to get the people ready, because He was coming to meet with them.

On the third day, God descended on Mount Sinai and spoke the Ten Commandments. Apparently, the style of His appearing was not what the people had in mind. They reacted in a "Fear Mountain" kind of way.

> *When the people saw the thunder and lightning and heard the trumpet and saw the mountain in smoke, they trembled with fear. They stayed at a distance and said to Moses, "Speak to us yourself and we will listen. But do not have God speak to us or we will die." Moses said to the people, "Do not be afraid. God has come to test you, so that the fear of God will be with you to keep you from sinning." The people remained at a distance, while Moses approached the thick darkness where God was.* (Exodus 20:18–21)

To me, this is one of the saddest stories in the Bible. The mighty God who saved His children by dividing the Red Sea had come to interact with them, but instead of receiving Him with excitement, they requested that He speak through an intermediary. All the smoke, thunder, and lightning had scared them off. So, instead of communing with God, they avoided Him.

Not Moses. He reveled in the "special effects" and lined up for another ride!

The Israelites were not the first people to get their God signals crossed. The heaven-to-earth communication breakdown began in the garden when Adam and Eve sinned, covered themselves with fig leaves, and hid from their Maker. (See Genesis 3:1–8.) It would be thousands of years before Jesus would redeem His creation.

Like Moses, Jesus was born to deliver God's people from slavery. And, like Moses, He was born at a time when children were slaughtered in order to preserve the power of the slave drivers. There are other similarities between the prophet Moses and *the* Prophet, Jesus. Both entered the waters of baptism (one through the Red Sea and one in the river Jordan), symbolizing the death of the old order and the birth of the new. Both were tested and empowered in the wilderness, and both climbed mountains to commune with God. And, from mountains, both men commissioned the bringing of God's government to the earth.

In Moses' case, the commission was summarized in the Ten Commandments given by God. (See Exodus 20:1–17.) In Jesus' case, the commission—God's new order of thinking and living—was brought to light in the Beatitudes, which Jesus preached as part of His Sermon on the Mount.

> *When Jesus saw the crowds, he went up on a mountainside and sat down. His disciples came to him, and he began to teach them. He said: "Blessed are the poor in spirit, for theirs is the kingdom of heaven. Blessed are those who mourn, for they will be comforted. Blessed are the meek, for they will inherit the earth. Blessed are those who hunger and thirst for righteousness, for they will be filled. Blessed are the merciful, for they will be shown mercy. Blessed are the pure in heart, for they will see God. Blessed are the peacemakers, for they will be called children of God. Blessed are those who are persecuted because of righteousness, for theirs is the kingdom of heaven."*   (Matthew 5:1–10)

Jesus revealed God's kingdom in a new way. When He said *"Blessed are…,"* it essentially meant "Happy are…." Notice that Jesus proclaimed the "be attitudes" and not the "do attitudes." He strapped in His hearers for a ride on "Fun Mountain" and guided their roller coaster through the old covenant—but with a new twist.

The Pharisees probably felt like vomiting when Jesus called everyone to be more righteous than the teachers of the law. (See Matthew 5:20.) Imagine how the people's stomachs dropped when they learned that their words could murder people and their thoughts could fornicate. (See Matthew 5:21–22, 27–28.) How upside-down they must have felt when Jesus told them to love their enemies and to pray for their persecutors! (See Matthew 5:43–48.) You can almost hear the religious-minded screaming in horror as Jesus taught them to approach God personally as *"our Father in heaven."* (See Matthew 6:9.)

Once again, God invited His people on the ride of their lives—not down easy street but on a course He knew they could not navigate in their own strength. There would be plenty of ups and downs and lots of unexpected twists and turns. All these things would position them to accept His grace. They had only to strap themselves in and throw their hands up in surrender. Then He would empower them to do the impossible.

Tickets for Fun Mountain are still available. The ride is often rocky but always joyful. I guarantee that it will be the ride of your life.

Created with Purpose and Destiny

When God gives an invitation, you know He has something specific in mind. Everything He creates and everything He does comes preloaded with purpose—no matter what it looks like and no matter what your response is to it. When God descended upon Mount Sinai, He had more planned than the people realized. His intent reached all the way to the Sermon on the Mount…and beyond. The Mosaic covenant was a revelation of something new, and it positioned God's people for another shift yet to come.

For God, the creation of something (such as a new order, a function of nature, a person, or an opportunity) and the establishment of its purpose are not separate things. The creation account illustrates what I mean.

> God said, "Let there be light," and there was light. God saw that the light was good, and he separated the light from the darkness. God called the light "day," and the darkness he called "night." And there was evening, and there was morning—the first day.   (Genesis 1:3–5)

Notice that God not only created the light, but He also "saw" the light. The Hebrew word translated "saw" is ra'ah.[1] It means that God did more than look at the light; He looked into it. For Him, the light and its purpose were inseparable. When He saw the light, it became its purpose, and He called it "day." God's seeing the light's purpose and destiny was His reason for naming it.

Think about this in terms of prophecy. God created you in His image and likeness. (See Genesis 1:26–27.) You were in Christ from the foundation of the world. (See Ephesians 1:3–4.) He saw you before your mother saw you and before your father's eye twinkled with thoughts of you. God named you before your parents did. Yes, you were in Him from the foundation of the world. Your purpose and your destiny were in Him all that time, too—but when God saw them, they became what He intended.

God looked into the purpose and destiny of every aspect of His creation; He called it, and it became what He purposed. He created us to do the same. For example, Adam did this when he named the animals. (See Genesis 2:19.) In naming them, he called out the potential within them. After the fall, Adam was unable to perceive the creation in this way, and he was powerless to call out its potential. No wonder Scripture says that the creation is groaning with birth pangs and is eagerly awaiting the manifestation of the children of God. (See Romans 8:19–22.) It is as if the universe is in labor, and it will continue to be so until God's people—the ones who know their identity—recognize its purpose and release the destiny God intended for it.

Understanding your destiny is important, but knowing your identity empowers you to achieve that destiny. People everywhere ask, "What's my destiny?" but they overlook the more important issue. If I could tell you your destiny, it would mean little until you knew who you were and where you came from. Only then would you see where you were going. As long as your identity is unclear, you may try to reach your destination, but you will be limited to earthly means. That is a problem, because your destiny in God exceeds earthly boundaries and resources. You were born on the earth, but you came from heaven.

Common sense says that in order to get to a specific location, you must first correctly identify your starting point. Until you do, you are as good as lost. My Droid phone taught me that lesson by way of my stomach. The phone's GPS tool was fantastic. I could travel almost anywhere in the States and find my favorite restaurant, Buffalo Wild Wings. It was easy: I'd hit the icon, and—*bam!*—the scent of Mango Habanero sauce filled the air.

On one trip, I deplaned and forget to switch my phone out of airplane mode. I did *not* forget to look up my favorite wing joint. But when I tapped the GPS function, the little circle on my screen just kept turning. Instead of getting a fix on my food, I got this disappointing message: "No location found."

Bummer, I thought. *What's wrong with this thing?*

God spoke to me right there and said, "That's where most people are. That's where most *Christians* are. They want to reach their destinies, but they don't know where they originate from. They don't know their identity."

Your spiritual GPS system is amazing, but if you don't know that you're a son or daughter of God, the little circle on the screen of your heart will just keep turning. You'll know you were created with a purpose, but the specifics will elude you. Even if you stumble upon your destiny, you won't recognize it. You could spend a lifetime striving to *get* what you already *are*.

The Best Title of All

My being called into prophetic ministry is better than anything I'd imagined while growing up. But striving for the destiny of prophet without understanding my identity as a son of God would be asking for a demotion. There is no title or position greater than *son of God* or *daughter of God.* If you are in Christ, that is how God sees you. From there, you can go anywhere.

Identity Crisis

The fall of humanity was a roller-coaster ride with no apparent upside. History's most brutal plunge separated man from God. Yet, what most of us have learned about this separation is inaccurate. We have learned that man disobeyed God, sin separated man from God, and God separated Himself from man. Only the first part of this is true. Man absolutely disobeyed God. But here is the rest of the story: *Man separated himself from God* because man was ashamed of his sin.

When Adam and Eve fell for the serpent's scheme and sinned (see Genesis 3:1–7), they immediately saw themselves in a new, unflattering light. So, they covered themselves with fig leaves and set a precedent that human beings would follow throughout history—they ran from God.

The man and his wife heard the sound of the LORD God as he was walking in the garden in the cool of the day, and they hid from the LORD God among the trees of the garden. But the LORD God called to the man, "Where are you?" He answered, "I heard you in the garden, and I was afraid because I was naked; so I hid." And he said, "Who told you that you were naked? Have you eaten from the tree that I commanded you not to eat from?" (Genesis 3:8–11)

Adam and Eve were ashamed; therefore, they became afraid. The idea of shame was foreign but devastating; it instantly distorted their vision. They had traded in their "God glasses" for a superficial kind of seeing that judged outward appearances alone. Instead of seeing in themselves the image and likeness of God, they saw only nakedness. It would take time for all the repercussions to play out. Death, sickness, and more bad choices would show up soon enough, but the fracture in their souls was already apparent.

Just as the soul is composed of three parts (mind, will, and emotions), three areas of Adam and Eve's vision were impaired: how they saw God, how they saw themselves, and how they saw others. Their primary focus was now on *self*. They looked at their "nakedness" and became chronically self-absorbed. This was contrary to the Maker's design. He had not created them for themselves or for their own pleasure. But sin, which is inherently selfish, entangled them in navel-gazing.

What a blow it must have been! Their perspective had been turned inside out and upside down. Created by God in wholeness, their minds had been perfectly sound. They had seen God as He was. Therefore, they had seen themselves and each other as He saw them. But now, the lens was cracked. Everything looked different.

All human senses were negatively affected by the fall of humanity. Among other forms of impairment, the ability to taste was diminished, the facility of sight was compromised, and the capacity to hear God and others through a pure heart was lost. Emotions became twisted, so that human beings felt things God never intended them to feel. Instead of feeling secure and confident, they were burdened with shame and regret. God had not designed them to experience either!

Second Corinthians 7:10 says, "*Godly sorrow brings repentance that leads to salvation and leaves no regret, but worldly sorrow brings death.*" Why? Because regret drags you back to your past. It is a place that doesn't exist, a place God does not see. You were not created to dwell in the past. You were created to acknowledge the effect of your choices, to choose a better direction, if necessary, and to exit the past. That is what repentance really is—a consciously made U-turn.

From the garden of Eden to the garden tomb, emotions such as shame, guilt, and remorse kept humanity in spiritual stocks and chains. Adam and Eve lost the clear conscience they had once enjoyed. Instead of walking boldly and confidently before God, they shied away from the throne of grace. Instead of approaching the Father and allowing Him to wrap His arms around them, they disqualified themselves and did without His love.

It was a recipe for disaster. God never intended His children to respond to Him in this way. He created them to commune with Him freely.

He purposed to continually refresh them with words of destiny. Now, they interpreted their shame as a barrier to a relationship with Him. Shame stripped away their confidence in His commitment to their well-being.

We were created to *"draw near to God with a sincere heart and with the full assurance that faith brings, having our hearts sprinkled to cleanse us from a guilty conscience and having our bodies washed with pure water"* (Hebrews 10:22). Although sin drained away our confidence before God and tempted us to hide from Him, it could not change *His* heart! God remained (and still remains) willing to step down into our sinful and naked state. He proved His willingness in the garden of Eden. When Adam and Eve sinned, He reached out as any loving Father would. His first words were not "How could you be such an idiot?" Rather, His first words were *"Where are you?"* (Genesis 3:9). The Father did not scatter His children; He gathered them. He spoke prophetically to their fallen hearts and promised the restoration to come. (See Genesis 3:15.)

The Womb of Heaven

God did not suspend His love for Adam and Eve due to their failure. Neither did He shy away from Abraham, whose attempts at self-preservation included allowing his wife, Sarah, to be handed over to strange men. (See Genesis 12:10–20; Genesis 20.) And when Moses murdered an Egyptian in his zeal to protect an Israelite, God did not write him off. (See Exodus 2:11–3:22.) God *never* suspends His love for His kids.

David knew this truth more than most people did. Even after he had committed adultery and added murder to his résumé, God continued to love His chosen king. (See 2 Samuel 11:1–12:24; Psalm 51.) David's psalms show how he availed himself of God's perfect love, which cast out his earthly fears. Even though David may have believed he had been conceived in sin (see Psalm 51:5), he learned that he was *"fearfully and wonderfully made"* (Psalm 139:14) by God. He understood the great care with which God had knit him together in his mother's womb. (See Psalm 139:13–15.) He learned to value his unique identity and to rejoice in the fact that he was one of a kind.

This awareness enabled David to stand against Goliath on his own terms. When King Saul tried to dress David in the king's armor, David said, in effect, "No way. It doesn't fit me. Let me fight the giant my way." With five stones and a slingshot, David ran straight at the warrior who had terrorized Israel's entire army and slew him! (See 1 Samuel 17:32–51.)

How could a young man who had suffered so much rejection become so bold? He had allowed God to nurture him in His presence. In that environment, David became himself—the uniquely powerful, bold, confident leader God had created him to be. Worship took David to the place where he was with God before the foundation of the earth, long before His father, Jesse, was even born. There, he was, in essence, unscathed by events in his natural lifetime and removed from even the reach of the fall.

In worship, David entered the womb of heaven, the place of his origin, where he had a clean slate and a healthy self-image. There, he could believe everything God said about him. In heaven's womb, a wounded soul became David, a son of God and the king of Israel.

Pathways of Righteousness

Let's take another look at the spiritual confidence described in Hebrews 10:

Therefore, brothers and sisters, since we have confidence to enter the Most Holy Place by the blood of Jesus, by a new and living way opened for us through the curtain, that is, his body, and since we have a great priest over the house of God, let us draw near to God with a sincere heart and with the full assurance that faith brings, having our hearts sprinkled to cleanse us from a guilty conscience and having our bodies washed with pure water. (Hebrews 10:19–22)

The blood of Jesus runs through our hearts and restores our confidence to enter the Most Holy Place. We can draw near to God because the blood cleanses our guilt and regret, and prophesies the end of our hiding! Through it, we can speak to the creation without feeling naked and ashamed. We can prophesy its purpose, not from behind our fig leaves but from our position with Christ.

We are *"the righteousness of God"* in Christ Jesus (2 Corinthians 5:21); therefore, we can go boldly before the throne of grace. When we make mistakes, we are to draw near to God. When we mess up, we are to draw near to God. When the accuser tells us to hide, we know better than to listen to him. We know that we are not called to be ashamed; we are called to climb up on Daddy's chair.

Before we continue in the book of Hebrews, let's look at Psalm 23, where David wrote of God, *"He restores my soul; He leads me in the paths of righteousness for His name's sake"* (Psalm 23:3 NKJV). This truth is so much bigger than we realize. When our souls are restored, we gain access to parts of our brains that were not previously accessible. Realms of the imagination are activated that have never been activated before, and new pathways emerge!

The writer of Hebrews compared the blood sacrifices of the earthly tabernacle with the shedding of Christ's blood. Hebrews 9 opens with a description of the annual sacrifice made by the earthly high priest for the people's sins. The chapter goes on to make the comparison with our new covenant reality:

> *The Holy Spirit was showing by this that the way into the Most Holy Place had not yet been disclosed as long as the first tabernacle was still functioning. This is an illustration for the present time, indicating that the gifts and sacrifices being offered were not able to clear the conscience of the worshiper. They are only a matter of food and drink and various ceremonial washings—external regulations applying until the time of the new order.* (Hebrews 9:8–10)

The tabernacle was meaningful, but its larger purpose was to prepare us for something much better.

> *But when Christ came as high priest of the good things that are now already here, he went through the greater and more perfect tabernacle that is not made with human hands, that is to say, is not a part of this creation.* (Hebrews 9:11)

"The greater and more perfect tabernacle" is the heavenly tabernacle that the earthly one foreshadowed. The blood of animals covered the people's sin for one year but never removed that sin. Jesus' blood cleansed us from the inside out, once and for all.

> [Christ] *did not enter by means of the blood of goats and calves; but he entered the Most Holy Place once for all by his own blood, thus obtaining eternal redemption. The blood of goats and bulls and the ashes of a heifer sprinkled on those who are ceremonially unclean sanctify them so that they are outwardly clean. How much more, then, will the blood of Christ, who through the eternal Spirit offered himself unblemished to God, cleanse our consciences from acts that lead to death, so that we may serve the living God!* (Hebrews 9:12–14)

The blood of Christ created a brand-new pathway of righteousness within us. It was a road not previously traveled. It not only gave us a new way to live, but it also opened our souls to a new way of being.

Our life experiences often create neuro-pathways in our brains that can later be activated by subsequent events, leading to physiological responses. If a particular smell—maybe the scent of the cologne your father used, or an aroma similar to that of the brownies your mother baked when you were little—has ever triggered a memory, you know what I'm talking about. For example, every time my wife hears a certain song, she is transported back to our honeymoon. The music fires up the neuro-pathway that was created during that time and brings the memories into the present.

In a comparable—but negative—way, sin creates its own "pathways," with sin-consciousness as their trigger. Our awareness of having committed a particular sin takes us back to a specific place in our conscience and makes us believe that we are still the person who committed that sin. However, the Bible refutes that sin-consciousness trigger. It says that the blood of Jesus *"cleanse[s] our consciences from acts that lead to death."* His blood leads us in brand-new paths of righteousness—He restores our souls.

The blood of Jesus creates new neuro-pathways called *righteousness*. As a result, we become conscious of His righteousness rather than of our sin. This affects how we see God, ourselves, and each other. When we are no longer sin-conscious, we don't hide from God; instead, we run to Him. We see ourselves as God sees us—through His Son's blood. We see one another through the blood, too. In other words, we see God's intent, and we think like heaven.

Consequently, when we see others through the prism of righteousness, we can prophesy to them clearly, without wearing any "fig leaves." We know it's not about us but about Jesus. So, we point to Him and say, "This is what God's path of righteousness looks like in your life"—and they will become that.

That kind of thinking comes straight from heaven.

Thinking like Heaven

1. Have you ever had a "Fear Mountain" reaction to God because He "showed up" in a way that was unexpected or uncomfortable for you? If so, what do you think His purpose was?

2. Ask God to show you one or more "be attitudes" to be happy in. What aspect of His response flips a switch in your thinking?

3. What questions, if any, have you already asked God about your destiny? How did His answers help to establish your identity? What new questions do you have? What is He saying to you today?

4. Describe your most recent "womb of heaven" experience, when you entered into the presence of God through worship and were nurtured by Him. What was birthed? What are you still waiting to "conceive"? Have you talked to God about it?

5. Ask God to show you someone who is experiencing failure or discouragement and is afraid to "ride" again. Then ask Him to give you the words to share that will help that person get back in line and "strap in" one more time.

Notes

1. *Biblesoft's New Exhaustive Strong's Numbers and Concordance*, s.v. "ra'ah" (OT 7200).

4

Out of Your Mind and into God's, Part 1

 Bob Hazlett @bob_hazlett
Intentionally choose to receive the mind of Christ instead of giving people a piece of yours. #ThinklikeHeaven

The mind works in amazing ways, especially when you are hungry or afraid. When I was a child, I loved Cracker Jacks, the caramel-coated popcorn in a box. My craving wasn't entirely for something sweet and salty. The truth is that I would have eaten almost anything to get to the prize at the bottom of the carton—which explains why I ate my sister's Cracker Jacks, too.

Hunger for a treat and a toy started my escapade. But once I knew I was busted, fear finished me off. There was no logical way to explain what I'd done, so when my father asked me what had happened, I spun a colorful yarn, saying, "I didn't do it! A flock of birds swooped down, stole the Cracker Jacks, and ate them. All they left was the prize!"

My father spoke sharply: "Are you making up stories again?"

My sister cut deeper: "Are you out of your mind?"

My creative storytelling was a lie based in fear. But not all storytelling is deceptive. Prophecy, for example, is the truthful telling of a story from God's perspective. As opposite as lying and prophecy are, they have one feature in common: Both require creative thought. To think like heaven is always a creative process. It takes you "out of your mind" and into the mind of Christ.

The Mind Transformed

Sometimes, when I want to clear my head, I drive to the beach. An uninterrupted view of the horizon seems to broaden my perspective, shrink my problems, and power up my prayers. For Jesus, mountains seemed to have a similar effect. He often climbed them so He could be alone with His Father.

Occasionally, Jesus took His disciples up a mountain with Him, as we see in this account from Matthew:

> *After six days Jesus took with him Peter, James and John the brother of James, and led them up a high mountain by themselves. There he was transfigured before them. His face shone like the sun, and his clothes became as white as the light. Just then there appeared before them Moses and Elijah, talking with Jesus.* (Matthew 17:1–3)

In the Greek, the word "*transfigured*" is *metamorphoo*,[1] the term from which our English word *metamorphosis* is derived. In Romans 12:2, the same word is translated "*transformed*":

Do not conform to the pattern of this world, but be transformed by the renewing of your mind. Then you will be able to test and approve what God's will is—his good, pleasing and perfect will.

Transformation reshapes temporal things to look like eternal ones. When Jesus was transfigured, His appearance was so changed that He resembled His heavenly surroundings. What the disciples saw was not a facsimile of Jesus but the true Jesus. Words could not describe the sight, so

Matthew used metaphorical language: *"His face shone like the sun, and his clothes became as white as the light"* (Matthew 17:2).

Jesus sometimes spoke in parables to convey in temporal language things that must be seen from an eternal perspective. He knew how heavenly concepts stretched the human mind. That is why He instructed the disciples not to discuss His transfiguration with anyone until after His resurrection. Earthly minds could not fathom the event until they had been resurrected in their thinking to perceive heavenly things.

Getting Out of Our Norms

Few things are more ingrained in earthly thinking than cultural norms and ethnic stereotypes. Like it or not, we naturally sort people into our mental pigeonholes. To think like heaven, we need to see human beings from a heavenly perspective. Paul understood this, and the transformation was already under way in his thinking when he wrote, *"Therefore, from now on, we regard no one according to the flesh"* (2 Corinthians 5:16 NKJV).

Whatever our race or ethnicity, we have been affected by the preconceived ideas of others. Jesus was no exception. People from Nazareth were looked down upon. When Philip told Nathanael about Jesus, Nathanael's bias showed in his question, *"Can anything good come out of Nazareth?"* (John 1:46 NKJV).

Gentiles had their share of detractors, too. Even after all that Jesus had taught him, Peter believed salvation was reserved for the Jews alone. He was clearly not thinking like heaven! So, one day, when Peter was good and hungry, God gave him a prophetic experience. Peter fell into a trance, saw heaven opened, and received a vision of unclean, nonkosher animals wrapped in what looked like a giant sheet. (See Acts 10:9–12.)

The Greek word for *"trance"* in Acts 10:10 is *ekstasis*, which literally means "a displacement of the mind."[2] Peter had to get "out of his mind" because Jesus was about to require of him something that even a hungry Jew would detest. Jesus said, *"Get up, Peter. Kill and eat"* (Acts 10:13). In other words, "Help yourself to some spareribs, lobster, and bacon."

"No way, Lord!" protested Peter. "I'm a good Jew. I never eat that stuff." (See Acts 10:14.)

For the record, I would have said, "Yes, Lord!" That buffet sounds better than anything I ever found at the bottom of a Cracker Jacks box.

Yet, to Peter, it was anathema. God had to pull the apostle out of his norms. He spelled out His intent, saying, *"Do not call anything impure that God has made clean"* (Acts 10:15). Whoa! Centuries of dietary laws went up in smoke, along with the Jews' distaste for Gentiles. But when Peter got to the bottom of what God had revealed, he found an unexpected prize—a new mind! God had used Peter's temporal state of hunger to draw him into an eternal perspective.

Jesus died so that all people—not just Jews—could experience the new birth. The idea was practically blasphemous to Peter. It took a supernatural, prophetic experience to rattle him *and* the church out of their religious cages. Unfortunately, because he feared the reactions of other Jewish believers, Peter soon relapsed into his old thinking and failed to establish the truth that God had revealed to him.

Revelation cannot produce transformation unless the revealed concept is established. It would take the apostle Paul to settle the issue. As a religious Jew and a scholar, Paul knew that Messiah would be *"a light for the Gentiles"* (Isaiah 42:6). Boldly, yet humbly, he confronted Jewish church leaders in regard to the Gentiles and specifically chastised Peter for caving in to social norms. (See Galatians 2:11–21.)

When the church got the Gentile issue right, it metamorphosed into the body that God intended it to be. This shows how important it is to be in God's mind and not our own, and it might explain the following admonition from Paul to his spiritual son Titus:

> *To the pure, all things are pure, but to those who are corrupted and do not believe, nothing is pure. In fact, both their minds and consciences are corrupted. They claim to know God, but by their actions they deny him. They are detestable, disobedient and unfit for doing anything good.*   (Titus 1:15–16)

Paul warned Titus to protect his thinking from temporal perspectives and earthly boxes, because what we think always determines how we act. Peter and others feared reprisals from other Jews. But Jesus had not come to establish a kingdom based in fear. He came to replace fear with a sound mind. (See 2 Timothy 1:7 NKJV, KJV.) He wanted people out of their minds, but not because of fear.

The mind of Christ is undisturbed. When we are in His mind, fear leaves, and the unseen is revealed. When He was transfigured, Jesus showed Peter what was available in the spiritual realm. He wanted Peter to taste and see God's goodness (see Psalm 34:8) and to know that heaven was open to him. It apparently worked, because one prophetic experience produced in Peter a spiritual hunger that led him to other supernatural experiences.

We are no different from Peter. God is stirring in us a hunger for heaven so that *we* will taste and see that He is good. He wants to take us out of our minds!

Fear, the Mind-Blower

The Bible teaches what modern science now confirms: Fear can cause you to "lose" your mind. "A study, done at the State University of New York at Buffalo by Zhen Yan, Ph.D., and colleagues and published in the journal 'Neuron,' showed that when your stress hormone cortisol spikes and then remains high, your prefrontal cortex is disturbed to the point that memory problems can occur."[3]

Seeing the Unseen

My wife, Kimberly, wears corrective lenses but still says that she does not see very well. What she means is that she is not a visual person. On a drive one day, I told her about an exercise I use to develop people's ability to "see" what is not there. It's simple: I describe a landscape scene with a waterfall and ask participants to add their own details to the picture. They soon realize that they see unseen things all the time. It is called *imagination*.

As we drove, Kim and I did the landscape exercise. When I asked her what she was seeing, she gave a surprising answer: "I don't see anything, but I feel the force of the waterfall on my skin. I guess I am more of a 'feeler.'"

Something even more surprising happened a few minutes later. Kim pointed to the sky and said, "Look at that cloud. It looks like a bunny rabbit!"

All I saw was a white puff in a sea of blue. But Kim saw a picture! She saw it because *we are all seers*. We use the eyes in our heads to see the temporal realm; we use the eyes of our hearts to see what is eternal. None of us sees things exactly the same way, but we are all capable of seeing.

When Paul shared with the Ephesian believers the nature of his prayers on their behalf, he talked about seeing the eternal:

> *I keep asking that the God of our Lord Jesus Christ, the glorious Father, may give you the Spirit of wisdom and revelation, so that you may know him better. I pray that the eyes of your heart may be enlightened in order that you may know the hope to which he has called you….*
>
> (Ephesians 1:17–18)

What Paul prayed for on behalf of the Ephesians is essential for us, as well. *"Heart"* here refers to "deep thought" or "imagination."[3] Your imagination is God-given; it is the channel through which you "see" His wisdom and all that He reveals. When the eyes of your heart are enlightened, you see things your physical eyes cannot detect, and you use your imagination to "view" them. God equipped you to see in this way.

Rabbi Moses Maimonides wrote about the role of the imagination in the prophetic:

> Prophecy is, in truth and reality, an emanation sent forth by the Divine Being through the medium of the Active Intellect, in the first instance to man's rational faculty, and then to his imaginative faculty; it is the highest degree and greatest perfection man can

attain; it consists in the most Perfect development of the imaginative faculty.[4]

The human imagination envisions what God communicates to the human spirit.[5] Divine words and impressions become pictures the heart can ponder and hold as spiritual reference points. When these unseen things of heaven are seen in the human heart, they pull us out of our minds and into God's. And when we get into God's mind, we see what He sees.

During His earthly walk, Jesus saw what God saw. When Philip first brought Nathanael to meet Jesus, it became clear that Jesus was a seer.

> When Jesus saw Nathanael approaching, he said of him, "Here truly is an Israelite in whom there is no deceit." "How do you know me?" Nathanael asked. Jesus answered, "I saw you while you were still under the fig tree before Philip called you."   (John 1:47–48)

Jesus got Nathanael's attention! Demonstrations like that always do. On a recent trip to Switzerland, I struck up a conversation with a young couple I met on a train. I told the man that I saw him taking a trip to Wales, where he would connect with people who would provide the resources and strategy for work he would be doing in Eastern Europe. Also, I shared that he would spend his time in Switzerland assembling a team that would go back and forth to Eastern Europe with him.

Both of their mouths fell open. The young man explained that he had just returned from Wales and had several trips to Eastern Europe lined up. The encounter opened the door to a deeper spiritual conversation, so we went to dinner and continued our talk. The couple asked me how I knew the things I had told them. My answer was simple: I didn't know these things; *I saw them*. It was like describing a scene from a movie or watching someone's vacation video on YouTube. All I did was share what I had seen.

The idea of seeing the unseen intrigued them. So, I gave them a practical example of how it works. As we dined, I noticed a shelf filled with wine bottles and pointed it out to them. It was near our table and had been there the whole time, but none of us had noticed it before. This showed how it is possible to see the unseen, while *not* seeing what is right before our eyes. The shelf of wine bottles was visible, but we had not turned our *attention* to it. Once we did, we became *aware* that it existed. And once we became aware, we began *accessing* the details: the types of wine on the shelf, the names on the bottles, the vintage years, and even the names of the bottle makers.

Let's take a look at how attention, awareness, and access relate to seeing the unseen.

Attention

Giving your attention is a decision that demands a change of focus. To pay attention to one thing, you have to minimize or eliminate your attention to something else. Colossians 3:1 tells us to pay attention to *"things above."* You cannot turn your focus upward and downward at the same time.

Do you remember when Peter walked on water during a storm? Jesus said, *"Come,"* and Peter obeyed. He set his focus on unseen things and experienced supernatural results. But when he turned his attention back to the storm, his walk on water ended. (See Matthew 14:22–33.) Peter's lesson has practical *and* eternal implications. To think like heaven, we have to turn our attention to whatever God wants to reveal or to accomplish. And to see people as He sees them, we have to turn our attention to them.

Awareness

When the young couple I dined with asked how such detail was possible in prophecy, I said it was a matter of being aware of what already exists. Awareness is the cognizance of something that had not previously registered in your consciousness.

As paradoxical as it seems, distractions can often heighten awareness. They disrupt your train of thought, draw you out of "thinking as usual," and help you to see the unseen. One of the most productive distractions is daydreaming, which consumes one-third to one-half of your waking hours. This form of distracted focus can open you up to creative and prophetic thinking.

Check out what scientists say about daydreaming:

Many scientists argue that daydreaming is a crucial tool for creativity, a thought process that allows the brain to make new associations and connections....The daydreaming mind is free to engage in abstract thought and imaginative ramblings. As a result, we're able to imagine things that don't actually exist, like sticky yellow bookmarks.[6]

I am not endorsing daydreaming in the pews! But the principle is exactly right. You may have figured out the reference to "sticky yellow bookmarks." The rest of the story is amazing. You and your pastor will both love it.

On a Sunday morning in 1974, Arthur Fry sat in the front pews of a Presbyterian church in north St. Paul, Minn. An engineer at 3M, Fry was also a singer in the church choir. He had gotten into the habit of inserting little scraps of paper into his choir book, so that he could quickly find the right hymns during the service. The problem, however, was that the papers would often fall out, causing Fry to lose his place.

But then, while listening to the Sunday sermon, Fry started to daydream. Instead of focusing on the pastor's words, he began to mull over his bookmark problem. "It was during the sermon," Fry remembers, "that I first thought, 'What I really need is a little bookmark that will stick to the paper but will not tear the paper when I remove it.'" That errant thought—the byproduct of a wandering mind—would later become the yellow Post-it note, one of the most successful office products of all time.[7]

Fry's "wandering mind" became aware of what would be a landmark innovation. It seemed to come out of nowhere. In my opinion, some of what we call daydreaming is the "viewing" of prophetic thoughts and pictures. We are more receptive to receiving them when our brains are in "default," or resting, mode—when we are actively engaged in one activity while our minds are somewhere else.

You have probably experienced this condition many times. It can happen when you are driving a car or watching TV. You continue the activity, but your mind switches tracks and explores another place.

My wife calls it my "happy place." When I go there, my mind *is* wandering, but once I become consciously aware of the switch, my mind is not wandering anymore; it is being *directed*. This is when creative and prophetic pictures seem to come out of nowhere. Without any effort, parts of my brain that don't usually interact start communicating with one another. The new "chemistry" they create maximizes my creativity.

This is what I call *active listening*. It's a skill I use in conversation. While I am listening to what the other person is saying, I am also attentive to the Holy Spirit, and I become aware of what He wants to reveal or say. It is a creative process, but my imagination does not create the information. That comes from God. My imagination is the screen on which He projects what He sees and makes it visible to the eyes of my heart.

Productivity and the "Happy Place"

It's no coincidence that 3M (the Post-it Note company) creates an environment for creativity. Fry's aha moment produced "one of the top five best selling office supply products in the world."[8] The firm allows employees to spend 15 percent of their working hours on their own projects[9]—in other words, in productive daydreaming. To bolster creativity, they are encouraged to take relaxing walks or even to have a nap or to play a game of Ping-Pong.[10] The team works hard, plays hard, rests well, and creates revenue—big revenue.

Access

The third part of seeing comes when you explore what you have become aware of. Details begin to emerge, and your faith—"*the substance of things hoped for, the evidence of things not seen*" (Hebrews 11:1 NKJV, KJV)—becomes engaged. Dealing in the unseen realm requires faith. You have to believe what you are seeing! Hope allows you to see the unseen; faith allows you to access the details.

Sensing Without Seeing

Do you remember a childhood game called Red Light, Green Light? One person gets to play the "stoplight," and the rest of the players try to advance without being seen so that they can tag the stoplight.

To start, the moving children form a line about fifteen feet away from the stoplight, who then turns away from them and announces, "Green light!" The kids scurry toward the stoplight, knowing they must freeze when the stoplight announces "Red light!" and before he or she turns to face them. Anyone caught moving at that point is out of the game.

The idea is for the stoplight to sense what is happening behind his or her back. I'm not saying that Red Light, Green Light is heaven's game, but it does illustrate a God-given grace we all experience—sensing what we cannot see. Who hasn't "randomly" thought of someone and immediately received an unexpected phone call or e-mail from that person? Most of us have also been prompted to look in a certain direction (maybe while sitting in a coffee shop and reading a book) only to catch a perfect stranger staring at us—and quickly becoming embarrassed when discovered. These impressions are common, because we are equipped with natural and spiritual abilities to sense what we cannot see.

When I was young, I used to walk one mile to school and back each day. I like to tell my kids it was an uphill climb in the snow both ways, but they know better. What I can say is that I entertained myself the whole way by kicking a stone as far as I could and then walking to the stone's new location with my eyes closed. To make it really interesting and potentially survivable, I tried to do it without tripping, falling, or getting creamed by a car.

I was very committed to the stunt and got so good at it that I could walk almost half the way home with my eyes closed. It sounds silly and even dangerous, kind of like the people who navigate busy sidewalks and mall corridors while texting, only to walk into mailboxes or be filmed doing face-plants in fancy mall fountains. I am glad there is no videotape of my antics!

The point remains that when you close your eyes, your other senses become hyperaware. This is not true when you are texting; your eyes are *not* closed, and you are focused only on what you are typing and reading. But what happens with closed eyes tells us that human eyesight is not as straightforward as it seems. We know the eyes receive images, and the brain processes them, but we have two vision tracks—one conscious and one intuitive. The eyes see more than we realized!

Scientists, including Beatrice de Gelder, find that in certain tests blind eyes *see*. One phenomenon is known as blindsight. Some people who have suffered blindness due to brain damage seem to react to facial expressions that they cannot physically see by unconsciously imitating whatever expression is displayed.[11] The intuitive vision track is receiving visual stimuli, even though the conscious vision track is not functioning. This extreme example illustrates that we absorb and retain some visual information that never penetrates the conscious mind. In other words, we have information at our disposal that we have yet to use.

"Knowing" Without Knowing

We learned that when our souls are restored, we gain access to previously inaccessible parts of our brains. We also know that Jesus was aware of what various Jewish leaders were thinking and of what Peter and Judas would do before they did it. (See, for example, Mark 2:1–12; Matthew 26:33–34, 69–75; John 13:21–27; 18:1–3.)

Jesus gave us the Holy Spirit to remind us of things we already know and to tell us about things we do not know but need to know. (See, for example, John 14:26.) A general term that many people use to describe a sense that something might happen is *premonition*. The story I shared about my job description involved a spiritual "premonition"; God prepared me for an event I did not know was coming. He often gives me a heads-up about what is about to occur. It usually comes in the form of an impression, a dream, or a conversation that runs through my head before an important conference or private meeting. I have even listed events on my calendar before receiving any invitation. It is not wishful thinking; I already know that I will accept because God gave me the "knowing" in advance.

The fact that God does this is proof to me that He does the same—or is willing to do the same—for you. One word of caution: There is a difference between knowing and presuming, and there is a way to tell the difference. To judge whether an impression is from God, act on it (if it is for you alone) or ask about it (whether or not it involves other people). You will either find the premonition being confirmed or will discover the timing is not yet right. Or, you will realize that the idea is your own presumption. Through continued communion with God and practiced communication, it becomes easier to know the difference. I always try to put more faith in God's ability to speak to me clearly than I do in my ability to hear perfectly. He's a good Teacher and knows how to move me forward, whether I miss it or nail it.

There is another key to confirming a spiritual premonition: If it does not produce hope, either it is not from God, or you are viewing it from the wrong perspective. Ask Him to bring the matter into clear focus. He *wants* you to know what you need to know.

David's Prophetic Premonitions

King David was so out of his mind and into God's mind that he had a relationship with Messiah before Christ ever came to the earth. It is documented in the book of Psalms. In one passage, David heard Messiah say, *"My God, My God, why have You forsaken Me?"* (Psalm 22:1–2 NKJV). Hundreds of years later, Jesus spoke those words as He hung on the cross. (See Matthew 27:46; Mark 15:34.)

Premonitions, Peace, and Hope

Before He went to the cross, Jesus told His disciples that the Holy Spirit would teach them *"all things,"* which includes things they could not have known on their own.

The Advocate, the Holy Spirit, whom the Father will send in my name, will teach you all things and will remind you of everything I have said

*to you. Peace I leave with you; my peace I give you. I do not give to you
as the world gives. Do not let your hearts be troubled and do not be
afraid.*   (John 14:26–27)

Almost in the same breath, Jesus promised an atmosphere of peace—
not worldly peace, but heavenly peace—full of harmony, tranquility, safety,
welfare, and health. In this atmosphere, our emotions are not at war. It is also
the soil in which revealed things are planted. When you experience emotional turmoil, it is difficult to embrace brand-new information, but God's peace
surpasses even the most difficult situations. It is the perfect environment for
seeing the potentially negative things that are ahead because it allows you to
view them from God's perspective, which always produces hope.

Is it possible to maintain hope when negative events are ahead?
Imagine that you received the worst possible news about the nation's future: Government structures were about to collapse. All assets would be
transferred to other nations. Personal property would be confiscated.
Citizens would be taken captive by a terrorist state.

Would you have a sense of peace under such circumstances? Could
you? Would you be able to prophesy hope to others in the midst of your
sorrow?

This hypothetical scenario is not as bizarre as you might imagine.
Jeremiah found himself in exactly this predicament. Yet here is part of
what he prophesied:

This is what the LORD *says: "When seventy years are completed for
Babylon, I will come to you and fulfill my good promise to bring you
back to this place. For I know the plans I have for you," declares the*
LORD, *"plans to prosper you and not to harm you, plans to give you
hope and a future."*   (Jeremiah 29:10–11)

Much of Jeremiah's ministry was to reveal the downside of Judah's situation; Jeremiah did not spare the people the difficult news God told him
to share. Yet he also maintained hope and prophesied some good news.
Despite the reality of the people's exile, God showed them a picture of a
brighter future. He gave them something to live *from* until it manifested in
the natural realm.

I remember teaching a group of students about how God wants to show us the future. To help them experience the lesson, I told them to ask God to reveal four things: (1) a place to go, (2) the name of a person to pray for, (3) the color of the clothing the person would be wearing, and (4) what the person's need was.

It was a provocative assignment, but the students got the idea and began jotting down the impressions God gave them. One young lady noted a particular store logo, the name *Michele*, the color purple, and the words *painful wrist*.

She went to the store with that logo. After thirty minutes, she left discouraged, because she saw no one dressed in anything purple. While she was leaving the store, her phone rang. The caller ID read "Michele." It was her boss calling.

Excited, she answered the phone and said, "Hi, Michele! Are you wearing purple right now?"

Her boss replied with surprise, "Yes. Why?"

The young lady asked, "Is your wrist in pain?"

"Yes!" her boss exclaimed.

That call produced results that came straight from God's thinking. Michele was healed. The young lady who had prayed for her was launched on a powerful journey with the Holy Spirit. She knew firsthand that what Jesus promised was real—the Holy Spirit *would* teach her new things.

We were created to get out of our minds because we belong in God's mind. If we embrace the unseen—if we give it our attention, become aware, and access all that God reveals—we will find endless prizes, enough for everyone.

Thinking like Heaven

1. Ask God to show you an area of your life in which you have already experienced a "metamorphosis," or a change of "shape," that makes

you look more like God. Then ask Him to show you another area He wants to transform, and thank Him for doing it!

2. God showed Peter new things about heaven during Jesus' transfiguration and later, during the disciple's trance. Find a Scripture that describes heaven's features in earthly terms. Ask God to show you yourself in that setting. Write down all you see, hear, and experience. Remind yourself throughout the day that you are "seated in heavenly places." (See Ephesians 2:6.)

3. Allow God to break open your stereotypes and fears so you can reach out in love to people you once "regarded according to the flesh." (See 2 Corinthians 5:16 NKJV.) Give an encouraging or prophetic word to someone you would not normally approach.

4. Ask God to help you pay attention to, and be aware of, the "God moments" that present themselves in every conversation and encounter. Then act on whatever He reveals in those moments. Write down these testimonies for your own reference and for the purpose of encouraging others.

5. Ask God to show you someone whom you will meet later this week. Write down what He reveals about the following: (1) where you will meet the person, (2) the person's name, (3) what the person will be wearing, and (4) what prayer need the person will have. Then pay attention—and make a record of what happens.

Notes

1. *Biblesoft's New Exhaustive Strong's Numbers and Concordance*, s.v. "metamorphoo" (NT 3339).
2. Ibid., s.v. "ekstasis" (NT 1611).
3. "You're Not Losing Your Mind, You're Just Stressed Out!" ThirdAge.com, March 14, 2012, https://ca.shine.yahoo.com/blogs/healthy-living/8217-not-losing-mind-8217-just-stressed-165900265.html.
4. Moses Maimonides, *The Guide for the Perplexed* (Grand Rapids, MI: Christian Classics Ethereal Library), 363, http://www.ccel.org/ccel/maimonides/guide.pdf.
5. Bob Hazlett, *The Roar* (New Haven, CT: Future Coaching Publications, 2013), 110.
6. Jonah Lehrer, "Daydream Achiever," Life of the Mind, August 31, 2008, http://www.boston.com/bostonglobe/ideas/articles/2008/08/31/daydream_achiever/.
7. Ibid.
8. Daven Hiskey, "Post-it Notes Were Invented by Accident," Today I Found Out, http://www.todayifoundout.com/index.php/2011/11/post-it-notes-were-invented-by-accident/.
9. "Time to Think," 3M.com, http://solutions.3m.com/innovation/en_US/stories/time-to-think#.
10. Jason Gots, "Why Top Innovators Make Time to Waste Time," May 15, 2012, bigthink.com, http://bigthink.com/humanizing-technology/why-top-innovators-like-3m-make-time-to-waste-time.
11. "Blindsight," Through the Wormhole, DNA Tube, http://www.dnatube.com/video/28432/Blindsight-in-Through-the-Wormhole.

5

Out of Your Mind and into God's, Part 2

Bob Hazlett @bob_hazlett
Criticism and creativity take the same amount of energy, but the first is a poor use of imagination. #ThinklikeHeaven

↩ ⟲ ★ •••

When we get out of our minds and into God's, we break out of norms, "see" without physical eyes, and know things outside our natural knowledge base. The imagination is a *big* player, as we have seen. Now comes the fun part: rediscovering the "factory default" settings that make the youthful imagination stellar!

The heart is the seat of human desire, what we call the *will*. In chapter 4, we discussed the heart's creative capacity, which is the imagination. *Merriam-Webster's* dictionary defines *imagination* as "the ability to imagine things that are not real…to form a picture in your mind of something that you have not seen or experienced…to think of new things."[1]

The Bible also talks about "new things":

As it is written: "What no eye has seen, what no ear has heard, and what no human mind has conceived"—the things God has prepared for those who love him—these are the things God has revealed to us by his Spirit.   (1 Corinthians 2:9–10)

God has prepared new things *for us*. He prepared the human imagination, too. We know it exists, and we use it continuously, but we might not realize all that He designed it to do. This very important organ of the soul was created to think like heaven. I like to say that it can catapult you from a deep, dark cave to a panoramic alpine view.

Do you want to go there?

Caveman Mentality

Recently, I talked with one of my children about trying new things and taking risks. She and her friends had entered a season of new experiences: They were living on campus, launching careers, and starting families. She told me that when they talked among themselves about how their lives were changing, one friend suggested they watch a movie called *The Croods*.

Have you seen it? If not, consider this your spoiler alert! The movie is a parable that features a prehistoric family living in a cave. The father is Grug, a stubborn, risk-averse caveman who believes he has seen too much to change his ways now. Most of his neighbors have perished, but, through hypervigilance, Grug has kept his family alive. He wants to keep it that way, so he refuses to try new things or to take any risks at all, including leaving the cave.

A conversation between Grug and his son, Thunk, captures the mind-set:

GRUG

Tonight we'll hear the story of Krispy Bear. A long time ago, this little bear was alive. She was alive because she listened to her father and lived her life in routine and darkness and terror. So she was happy. But Krispy had one, terrible problem. She was filled with...curiosity....And one day, while she was in a tree, the curious little bear wanted to climb to the top....And no sooner than she climbed to the top, *she saw something new and died.*

THUNK

Just like that?

GRUG

Yes! Her last moments of terror still frozen on her face.[2]

Thunk's sister, Eep, is fed up with her father's rationale, but Thunk has been well-trained.

THUNK

(freaked out)

I get it, dad. I get it. *I will never do anything new or different.*

GRUG

Good man, Thunk.[3]

Soon, Grug's position as leader of the hunt is threatened by Guy, a prehistoric inventor who knows how to create fire. Through a series of confrontations and close calls, Grug eventually relents. He becomes more open to new ideas, and his family discovers a world more open and beautiful than they had dreamed possible.

The human imagination can and should inspire us, but the Croods parable shows how the imagination can be used to confine us in dark caves built with nothing more than our thoughts.

From Cave to Mountaintop

Even great men and women in the Bible battled their limited views of God and what He could do. Some of them, like David, lived in actual caves for a season. (See, for example, 1 Samuel 22:1–2.) Elijah hid in a cave when he fled from Jezebel. (See 1 Kings 19.) Others lived in metaphorical caves. Moses was in the latter category. As an infant, he was divinely spared death at the hands of Pharaoh—and was then raised in Pharaoh's own home. After Moses grew up, his roots and his calling prompted him to defend a Hebrew man who was being mistreated by an Egyptian. Moses killed the Egyptian, then fled the country.

He hid in Midian. His days of luxury were long gone. So was his self-confidence. For forty years, Moses lived in obscurity, until God broke into his "cave" and spoke to him from a burning bush. God had big plans in mind: Moses was to deliver the Israelites from the current pharaoh's hand! Moses deferred. "Who am I to go to Pharaoh?" he asked. "I can't even speak well." (See Exodus 2–3.)

God understood the cave Moses was stuck in and was patient with him; He encouraged Moses, taught him, and led him as he led Israel. The two developed a brilliant relationship that carried Moses through the high points, as well as the lowest of lows. One of Moses' most dramatic experiences happened way up on Mount Sinai (Mount Horeb). Previously, Moses had asked God to reveal Himself.

> *Moses said, "Now show me your glory." And the* Lord *said, "I will cause all my goodness to pass in front of you, and I will proclaim my name, the* Lord, *in your presence. I will have mercy on whom I will have mercy, and I will have compassion on whom I will have compassion. But," he said, "you cannot see my face, for no one may see me and live." Then the* Lord *said, "There is a place near me where you may stand on a rock. When my glory passes by, I will put you in a cleft in the rock and cover you with my hand until I have passed by. Then I will remove my hand and you will see my back; but my face must not be seen."* (Exodus 33:18–23)

On Mount Sinai, God revealed His glory to Moses:

> *Then the* Lord *came down in the cloud and stood there with him and proclaimed his name, the* Lord. *And he passed in front of Moses, proclaiming, "The* Lord, *the* Lord, *the compassionate and gracious God, slow to anger, abounding in love and faithfulness, maintaining love to thousands, and forgiving wickedness, rebellion and sin."* (Exodus 34:5–7)

All told, Moses spent nearly eighty days on that mountain, on two separate occasions. God's presence was so profound that Moses took no food or water the whole time! (See Exodus 34:28.) On his first visit, God gave him the Ten Commandments and promised a plan for His earthly tabernacle. Moses saw what no human eye had seen before—the heavenly tabernacle. God gave him intricate instructions to build a replica so that the unseen God could visit man on the earth. As God revealed the structure and the furnishings of the tabernacle, He told Moses, *"See to it that you make them according to the pattern which was shown you on the mountain"* (Exodus 25:40 NKJV).

The writer of Hebrews later called the earthly tabernacle a *"copy and shadow"* of heavenly things.

There are priests who offer the gifts according to the law; who serve the **copy and shadow of the heavenly things**, as Moses was divinely instructed when he was about to make the tabernacle. For He said, "See that you make all things according to the pattern shown you on the mountain." (Hebrews 8:4–5 NKJV)

Moses returned from the mountain in the power of God, ready to implement His plan for the tabernacle. From a natural perspective, building such a heavenly structure on earth would be impossible under the best circumstances. Doing so in the wilderness would be like trying to download the 3-D version of The Lord of the Rings trilogy using a dial-up connection! Fortunately, God had promised Moses artisans who would have a full heavenly anointing to build on earth what he had seen in heaven. (See Exodus 31:1–11.)

The earthly structure had to include all the sights, sounds, and scents of heaven. The skilled workers became a Holy Spirit-inspired panel of fashion designers, furniture makers, architects, metalworkers, jewelers, and a variety of other craftspeople.

Moses said to the children of Israel, "See, the LORD has called by name Bezalel the son of Uri, the son of Hur, of the tribe of Judah; and He has filled him with the Spirit of God, in wisdom and understanding, in knowledge and all manner of workmanship, to design artistic works, to work in gold and silver and bronze, in cutting jewels for setting,

*in carving wood, and to work in all manner of artistic workmanship.
And He has put in his heart the ability to teach, in him and Aholiab
the son of Ahisamach, of the tribe of Dan. He has filled them with
skill to do all manner of work of the engraver and the designer and the
tapestry maker, in blue, purple, and scarlet thread, and fine linen, and
of the weaver; those who do every work and those who design artistic
works."* (Exodus 35:30–35 NKJV)

It was a supernatural undertaking. Moses' imagination was imprinted
with the heavenly images God had showed him. Now it was left to Moses
to impart the revelation to creative people so that their imaginations would
be activated, too.

God took Moses a long way from the "cave" called *Midian*.

Caves, Valleys, and Mountains

David lived through his share of highs and lows, and his many psalms
chronicle his journey. According to some biblical scholars, Psalms 15
through 24 constitute a "relatively self-contained" collection arranged to
be read in the order presented.[4] Three of them—Psalms 22, 23, and 24—
track David's emotional path from cave to valley to mountaintop.

In Psalm 22, David described the life of a man persecuted nearly to the
point of death. *"Many bulls surround me; strong bulls of Bashan encircle me.
Roaring lions that tear their prey open their mouths wide against me"* (Psalm
22:12–13). David was accustomed to being persecuted and tormented by
the envious King Saul, who wanted him dead. At one point, he went to
Gath, where still another king made him afraid. *"So [David] pretended to
be insane in their presence; and while he was in their hands he acted like a mad-
man, making marks on the doors of the gate and letting saliva run down his
beard"* (1 Samuel 21:13). When David left Gath, *"he escaped to the cave of
Adullam"* (1 Samuel 22:1). The fearless slayer of Goliath often felt isolated
and forgotten. Yet, even in the dire situation he described in Psalm 22,
David continued to praise and worship God.

In Psalm 23, David described walking through an experience that felt
like death—he called it *"the valley of the shadow of death"* (Psalm 23:4 NKJV,

KJV). Once again, David continued to praise God and to express his trust in Him, saying, "*Surely goodness and mercy shall follow me all the days of my life; and I will dwell in the house of the LORD forever*" (Psalm 23:6 NKJV).

Because David had learned to worship God in the midst of these "cave" and "valley" situations, he could climb the "mountain" described in Psalm 24. This is where he began to get heaven's perspective of earth. He opened with a brilliant assessment: "*The earth is the LORD's, and everything in it, the world, and all who live in it*" (Psalm 24:1). He continued with an audacious question: "*Who may ascend the mountain of the LORD? Who may stand in his holy place?*" (Psalm 24:3).

Thinking like heaven compels us to ask heaven-sized questions, such as "Who can stand in God's holy place of authority over the earth?" Just when you might expect a heavenly "LOL! How could *you* expect to stand on *My* mountain?" an even more mind-boggling declaration is given in response: "Not just one person can stand here, but an entire generation *will* stand here! It is a generation with clean hands, a pure heart, and an uncompromising soul. Those in that generation will seek My face and open the way for the King to enter the gates of the earth!" (See Psalm 24:4–7.)

David was talking about *us*. Because Jesus was victorious over His valley, and because He conquered His cave, we, too, will traverse the valley of death and survive the cave of darkness to climb the mountain of God. We will be a generation of believers whose hands are clean, whose hearts are pure, and whose souls are whole. We will be heaven-ascenders, heaven-askers, and heaven-bringers, so that the King of Glory may come in!

The 411 on Imagination

The human imagination has gotten a bad rap. We are too quick to shoot down other people's dreams. To those with God-given visions, we often shake our heads in disbelief and say, "Dude, you're dreaming. That idea is all in your imagination!"

Until they are made manifest, our dreams *are* in our imaginations. That is where they are supposed to begin. I am not saying that every dream is a God-idea. The imagination *can* lead where God would never send us. But it can also take us to where He is. So, let's get the lowdown on what C. S. Lewis called our "organ of meaning."[5]

Imagination, Fantasy, and Worry

To understand what imagination is, we need to eliminate what it isn't. *Imagination is not fantasy.* Fantasy always puts *us* at the center of the story. If I were to fantasize about the days of King Arthur's court, guess who would play the knight in shining armor? You guessed right: Sir Bob would swoop down, rescue the damsel in distress, and save the kingdom. Why? Because fantasy is based in the old nature.

C. S. Lewis distinguished between fantasy and imagination in his book *Surprised by Joy.* He talked about when he and his brother were young and created a fictional world called Animal-Land. Lewis said his hours spent imagining Animal-Land were not focused on *self*; they were practice for becoming a writer. He admitted to having his share of fantasies, in which he saw himself "cutting a fine figure." But he said of those experiences, "I was training myself to be a fool."[6]

The apostle Paul instructed us to use our minds wisely:

> Be not conformed to this world: but be ye transformed by the renewing of your mind, that ye may prove what is that good, and acceptable, and perfect, will of God. For I say, through the grace given unto me, to every man that is among you, not to think of himself more highly than he ought to think; but to think soberly....
>
> (Romans 12:2–3 KJV)

Another misunderstanding concerning the imagination involves its use. Worry is not God's intended purpose for your imagination. Worry is a *misuse* of it. Hope uses the imagination to expect the best; worry uses it to conjure up worst-case scenarios. That is why Paul said we are to be "*casting down imaginations, and every high thing that exalts itself against the knowledge of God, and bringing into captivity every thought to the obedience of Christ*" (2 Corinthians 10:5 KJV).

The Faith of Imagination

Do you remember when Jesus got inside Nicodemus's head? Jesus explained unseen things to a man who relied heavily on his intellect and his physical senses. Nicodemus was spiritually hungry for something Jesus had, but he could not fathom what it was. Jesus recognized his hunger but had to get through the walls of his "cave." The shingle outside that cave read NICODEMUS: "ISRAEL'S TEACHER." But Jesus talked about things that could not be grasped intellectually, and He explained why Nicodemus was baffled, saying,

> *Very truly I tell you, we speak of what we know, and we testify to what we have seen, but still you people do not accept our testimony. I have spoken to you of earthly things and you do not believe; how then will you believe if I speak of heavenly things? No one has ever gone into heaven except the one who came from heaven—the Son of Man.*
>
> (John 3:11–13)

In our vernacular, I think Jesus was saying, "There are things you must see to believe. Heaven is full of them, but you must come *from* heaven to see them." The redeemed imagination sees heavenly things by faith. By faith, we get into God's mind. Then we can download the pictures He wants to show us.

The Atmosphere of Imagination

Imagination needs the right atmosphere in order to flourish. Caves need not apply. Grug Crood became a prisoner of his cave and made his loved ones prisoners, too. It wasn't the physical cave that kept them locked up. Grug's rules did that. He was so preoccupied with *not dying* that neither he nor his family really *lived*.

Rules often hinder creative thinking. The law of Moses is a good example. It was given to show people what to think and how to act. In the end, due to the effects of the old nature, it showed only that their thoughts and actions were wrong. Spiritually speaking, it was "death by a thousand rules." That is why Paul wrote,

Through Christ Jesus the law of the Spirit who gives life has set you free from the law of sin and death. For what the law was powerless to do because it was weakened by the flesh, God did by sending his own Son in the likeness of sinful flesh to be a sin offering....Those who live according to the flesh have their minds set on what the flesh desires; but those who live in accordance with the Spirit have their minds set on what the Spirit desires. The mind governed by the flesh is death, but the mind governed by the Spirit is life and peace. (Romans 8:2–3, 5–6)

It is paradoxical in a heavenly way: Moses received the law on the mountain, but it was fulfilled when Jesus came out of a cave—*His grave.* Once we have been raised with Christ, our thinking is also resurrected. (See Colossians 3:1.) Paul drove home this point in relation to Gentile believers who kept a different Sabbath day and ignored Jewish dietary laws. In Romans 13 and 14, Paul explained that Jesus fulfilled the law of Moses and instituted the law of love, which fulfills all the commandments.

Paul demolished the cave of rules and religious-mindedness, writing, *"The kingdom of God is not a matter of eating and drinking, but of righteousness, peace and joy in the Holy Spirit"* (Romans 14:17).

Confidence, Peace, and Happiness

The atmosphere you become aware of will help determine the thought you arrive at. Intense focus helps to bring recollection of facts you already know. However, brain researchers have observed that an atmosphere of unfocused rest may provide the place for aha moments—those creative moments when we have thoughts we have never had before. Such moments could happen during worship, spiritual "soaking," or just resting in God's presence.

An atmosphere of rest is produced by confidence, peace, and happiness. Proverbs 28:1 says that *"the righteous are as bold as a lion."* When the human conscience is clean, our confidence before God is strong. When we are fearful, or when we believe that God is mad at us, we frustrate our ability to hear from heaven. Peace helps us to hear freely from heaven.

This explains why I hear God best in the shower! A shower relaxes me. So does laughter. When we are restful and peaceful, we feel safe and happy. We become more confident and open to new ways of thinking and of doing things. This idea applies to more than our creative exploits. It should also adjust our views about church. Sometimes, we think we are going to church solely to hear a sermon, so we become impatient when the worship portion of the service lasts longer than usual. We wonder why the pastor doesn't give the worship team "the hook" and just start preaching.

That is a cave-dweller mentality. It makes assumptions that have nothing to do with God or heaven, and it dulls our hearts to the sound of God's voice. We *should* value preaching; but let's not go to church only to hear sermons. Let's go to worship God and let Him decide how He will speak to us. Then we will hear what we have never heard before.

Isn't that what we really want?

Reclaiming Your Lost Artist

There is an artist in you. Reading that statement might make your heart leap with hope, or it might make you squirm. Both responses speak to uncertainty about your creative nature. The childhood version of you never doubted your creativity; the adult model probably does. It is likely that by the time you completed grade school, you had learned to reserve the word *artist* for only certain types of people.

Jesus entreated us to be more childlike. Notice what He did when His disciples asked Him who ranked highest in the kingdom of heaven:

> He called a little child to him, and placed the child among them. And he said: "Truly I tell you, unless you change and become like little children, you will never enter the kingdom of heaven."
>
> (Matthew 18:2–3)

Jesus had a knack for making perplexing statements. Wrapped in this one is a key to living as God intended. For those of us who are adults, it forces a change in how we think and act. Many of us have worked hard to leave behind the child in us. Jesus frowns upon the idea, because the childlike are better equipped to grow in His kingdom.

This is obvious on a practical level. Children have not developed the extensive set of judgments that adults have, so they are open to things that seem outside adult norms. Their openness frees them to use their inherent potential and be creative. For example, just watch a child with a coloring book. Most children have no problem coloring outside the lines or making someone's eyes an unusual color, such as orange.

Artist Pablo Picasso was an adult who "colored outside the lines." He did not let physical dimensions dictate his rendering of people or objects. In his Cubist work, all the angles are seen at once, even the ones that "should" be hidden from view. Critics ridiculed the approach, but Picasso kept painting. He apparently understood the importance of being childlike and the danger in becoming too adult-minded. A quote attributed to him reads, "Every child is an artist. The problem is how to remain an artist once he grows up."[7]

So, what do child artists look like? They look free! When they don't know an answer, they make up their own. If they can't understand the lyrics to a song, they make no excuses for writing their own words.

Being comfortable with such improvisation is good. Sometimes, when we hear God's voice, it feels as if we are "making up the lyrics" anyway—and for good reason: We have never heard such things before. *They are new to us and beyond our judgments.*

Like children, we have a lot to learn, and the artist within us likes it that way. So, let's rediscover that artist and have some fun. (No finger painting required.)

The Gift of Childlikeness

Getting to the artist within us is simple, according to psychologists Darya L. Zabelina and Michael D. Robinson of North Dakota State University. It begins with what children love most: *playing.* Zabelina and Robinson claim that children see tasks as "opportunities for play and exploration. The mindset of adults, on the other hand, is likely to involve trying to find the 'correct' conventional solution to a presented task or problem."[8]

Adults might make better decisions than children, but they sacrifice originality and creativity, according to Zabelina and Robinson. The researchers suggest, however, that it is "quite possible to facilitate a child-like mindset even among adults. If so, thinking of oneself as a young child for some period of time may facilitate creative performance."[9]

To prove their point, Zabelina and Robinson randomly separated a group of seventy-six undergraduates into two sections. Both sections were scheduled to take a creative-thinking test and were asked to write about what they would do if classes were canceled for the day. However, in one of the sections, the students were asked to imagine themselves as seven-year-old children. This group answered the questions more creatively and produced more original answers.[10] Even *imagining* themselves as children freed up their thinking!

Not all differences between adults and children are related to learning. Something happens to our brains when we age. One of the last areas of our brain to develop is the dorsolateral prefrontal cortex, or DLPFC. It works a little like the electronic collar used to keep dogs from crossing an invisible "fence." When adults cross certain behavioral lines, the DLPFC "zaps" them with signals that inhibit socially unacceptable impulses. The function is important. Nobody wants to see a forty-year-old man stick a kernel of corn up his nose. But the signals that keep us from doing that keep us from maximizing our creativity, as well.

We can strike a balance between adult behavior and childlikeness by keeping our perspective tuned to heaven and remembering the things Jesus said about children. In addition to His earlier statement about being child-like, He said,

> Take heed that you do not despise one of these little ones, for I say to you that in heaven their angels always see the face of My Father who is in heaven. For the Son of Man has come to save that which was lost.
> (Matthew 18:10–11 NKJV)

Jesus gave children high spiritual marks. He came not only to take our sin but also to restore our childlike ability to see heaven. It is time to remove our zappers and cross the invisible fence. The realm of our invisible God is waiting.

The Gift of Improvisation

Kids love to improvise. They are not embarrassed to create situations and characters and to pretend things. The world of make-believe is their "happy place."

Again, hearing God's voice sometimes feels like make-believe. This is a normal feeling, such as when something new is created. Many artists, musicians, and performers sense it when they are creating. They call it "letting go," or "getting out of your head." It means suspending the filters that normally monitor your thoughts, words, and actions.

Dr. Charles Limb is a smart guy with an awesome job: He studies the brain waves of jazz musicians and rappers by strapping them into functional magnetic resonance imaging (fMRI) machines while they make music.[11] And he has made some interesting discoveries, according to a Johns Hopkins press release:

> The scientists found that a region of the brain known as the dorsolateral prefrontal cortex, a broad portion of the front of the brain that extends to the sides, showed a slowdown in activity during improvisation. This area has been linked to planned actions and self-censoring, such as carefully deciding what words you might say at a job interview. Shutting down this area could lead to lowered inhibitions, Limb suggests.
>
> The researchers also saw increased activity in the medial prefrontal cortex, which sits in the center of the brain's frontal lobe. This area has been linked with self-expression and activities that convey individuality, such as telling a story about yourself.
>
> "Jazz is often described as being an extremely individualistic art form…," says Limb. "What we think is happening is when you're telling your own musical story, you're shutting down impulses that might impede the flow of novel ideas."[12]

Science shows that we *can* shut down our filters, get out of our heads, and use our imaginations to see and to create, not only in jam sessions but whenever we choose.

My daughter participates in theater groups at school and in the community. She described some exercises they do to learn improvisational drama. (Amazingly, the concepts also apply to spontaneous prophecy.) First, you have to say *no* to your head (your filters). Second, you have to say *yes* to the first thing that comes to mind and speak it.

This reminds me of something Jesus said about how His disciples should respond to persecutors: *"Whenever you are arrested and brought to trial, do not worry beforehand about what to say. Just say whatever is given you at the time, for it is not you speaking, but the Holy Spirit"* (Mark 13:11). This is true in any situation that demands a spontaneous response, including prophecy. The first step is to open your mouth. You will never know whether it is God until you say it. And if you don't say it, no one else will know, either.

Take some risks. Let go. Get out of *your* head. Improvise!

The Gift of Ignorance

There's a lot that kids don't know. It rarely bothers them, however. When they don't know the answer to a question, most kids do the best they can and say whatever comes to mind. A teacher once shared a student's response to a typical math question: *Daniel has 55 candy bars and eats 30 of them. What does Daniel have left?*

The student answered, "Diabetes."

It was a creative response! Kids have a gift for connecting their thoughts in unusual ways. As we get older, we don't like making mistakes, so we stick with what we know and are careful not to bump into the wrong answers. The downside is that what we know often keeps us from discovering *what we need to know*. Most young people have the opposite approach—they have not yet decided what the right answers are, so they bump into valuable new ideas all the time.

The freedom to make mistakes is a boon to creativity. No wonder young people are so imaginative—history shows that many inventors, artists, and pioneering thinkers have breakthroughs during their younger years. However, I don't believe we have to lose creativity as we age. We just need to be reminded of how to create.

Historical examples are important, but they reflect only natural patterns. When we think like heaven, we operate supernaturally. Our creativity is not limited to a certain season of life. Instead, it is a mind-set. Even a young man can grow old in his thinking, as Jesus' conversations with a certain young man proved. The exchange started when the man asked Jesus an important question: "*Teacher, what good thing must I do to get eternal life?*" (Matthew 19:16).

When Jesus answered with a checklist of commandments, the man insisted that he had obeyed all of them. Jesus then added, "*If you want to be perfect, go, sell your possessions and give to the poor, and you will have treasure in heaven. Then come, follow me*" (Matthew 19:21).

What happened next revealed the man's mind-set.

> *When the young man heard this, he went away sad, because he had great wealth. Then Jesus said to his disciples, "Truly I tell you, it is hard for someone who is rich to enter the kingdom of heaven."*
> (Matthew 19:22–23)

A careful reading of this passage tells us that this is more than a story about wealth; it is a story about maturity. The man is twice called a "*young man.*" The Greek word for that term describes someone who is not fully mature. In verse 21, Jesus challenged him to become "*perfect.*" In the Greek, the word used there is *teleios*, among whose meanings are "wanting nothing necessary to completeness," "full grown," and "mature."[13]

If you want to keep growing, you have to keep learning. A sign of maturity is the willingness to let go of what you have already learned in order to embrace what you *need* to learn. What this young man knew about the law of Moses and about his own lifestyle kept him from hearing what he needed to know. He was knowledgeable and wealthy, but he lacked the willingness to learn new things or to start a new life.

When I was learning to hear God's voice and to speak prophetically, God led me through a training exercise for a full year that kept me from getting too comfortable. I felt impressed that God wanted me to solely pray for and prophesy to children who were no older than ten. God's reason was not entirely clear to me, but I knew He was changing my thinking. I had to trust Him and allow the prophetic to flow creatively through me. It meant saying *yes* to whatever words came out of my mouth. I had to become like a child.

You might not be an improvisational rapper or a jazz musician, but you are an artist whose childlikeness has value. You are gifted with kingdom creativity. Your imagination is the canvas God will use to paint this world in the colors of redemption.

He is calling us out of the cave and onto the mountaintop.

Thinking like Heaven

1. Ask God to show you an area of "caveman" thinking in your life. What new things can you try in order to see something new?

2. Create a relaxed environment by, for example, going for a walk or taking a bath. Watch what God shows you; listen for His voice. As soon as possible, record what you have learned in your notebook or Tablet.

3. Imagine that you have a free day today. Take three to five minutes to write about what you will do with your time. Then imagine yourself as a seven-year-old with a free day, and write about your plans. What does a comparison of your responses reveal?

4. Think about the area in which you are strongest or most gifted. Now ask God to show you how to "forget" what you know so you can discover what you need to know. Take notes on what He reveals.

5. Try the following prophetic exercise with someone you meet this week. Start by saying, "When you were a kid, you really liked…" and let God fill your mouth with His answer.

Notes

1. Merriam-Webster.com, 2014, s.v. "imagination," http://www.merriam-webster. com/dictionary/imagination.
2. Kirk DeMicco and Chris Sanders, *The Croods*, Dreamworks Animation, 2012 (released 2013), Screenplay Explorer, http://screenplayexplorer.com/wp-content/scripts/croods.pdf. All emphasis is the author's.
3. Ibid.
4. See, for example, Philip Sumpter, "The Coherence of Psalms 15–24," *Biblica*, vol. 94, fasc. 2, Gregorian Biblical Press, 2013, 188, http://www.academia. edu/3848951/The_Coherence_of_Psalms_15_24_Gregorian_Biblical_ Press_2013_.
5. C. S. Lewis, *Rehabilitations & Other Essays*, C. S. Lewis Society of California, http://www.lewissociety.org/aboutus.php.
6. C. S. Lewis, *Surprised by Joy* (Orlando, FL: Harcourt, Brace, and Company, 1955), 15.
7. "Pablo Picasso Quotes," Goodreads, https://www.goodreads.com/author/ quotes/3253.Pablo_Picasso.
8. Darya L. Zabelina and Michael D. Robinson, "Child's Play: Facilitating the Originality of Creative Output by a Priming Manipulation," *Psychology of Aesthetics, Creativity, and the Arts* 4, no. 1 (2010): 61, American Psychological Association, http://www.psychologytoday.com/files/attachments/34246/ zabelina-robinson-2010a.pdf.
9. Ibid.
10. Ibid, 57.
11. Michelle Castillo, "Study: This Is Your Brain on Improv," Time.com, January 20, 2011, http://healthland.time.com/2011/01/20/study-this-is-your-brain-on-improv/#ixzz2lDg2QJWC.
12. "This is Your Brain on Jazz: Researchers Use MRI to Study Spontaneity, Creativity," February 26, 2008, http://www.hopkinsmedicine.org/news/ media/releases/this_is_your_brain_on_jazz_researchers_use_mri_to_study_ spontaneity_creativity. Press release quoted in Castillo, "Study: This Is Your Brain on Improv."
13. Blue Letter Bible, Greek Lexicon, s.v. "teleios" (*Strong's* NT 5046), https:// www.blueletterbible.org/lang/lexicon/lexicon.cfm?Strongs=G5046&t=NIV.

6

The Power of the Redeemed Soul

 Bob Hazlett @ bob_hazlett
Jesus died to save your spirit, heal your body, and
restore your soul. A restored soul is necessary for
understanding the supernatural, and it allows us to
hear God's voice more clearly. #ThinklikeHeaven
#RestoredSoul

As a boy, I wrestled with nightmares, fears, and dark thoughts that rico-cheted through my soul. One thought seemed too dark to mention. It came as a loud, recurring voice that said, "You are worthless. You need to take your own life."

The words haunted me, but I kept them to myself. When my night-mares were too scary to handle alone, I showed up in my parents' room. They knew I was struggling, so they would pray, "God, help Bob to think good thoughts. Help him not to have bad dreams."

That was our usual routine, after which I would return to my bed and try to think about nice things. But one night, the routine changed. I woke my parents and climbed in bed between them. My dad started off praying in the usual way. Then, suddenly, there was a shift. I heard a new authority in Dad's voice as he said, "These suicidal thoughts have to leave, in Jesus' name."

Something inside me broke in that instant, and I never had suicidal thoughts again—until a couple of years ago, during a series of meetings in Michigan. It happened one day when there was no afternoon session, and I was walking through the empty church building. There wasn't a soul in sight, but I heard a voice from the balcony, saying, "You are worthless. Kill yourself."

I stopped walking and looked up in the direction of the voice. Anyone watching me would have thought I was crazy as I spoke to the balcony, "I know who you are, and you are not my voice. You are not the voice of my Father, either. You are the voice of the accuser, and you have no power over me anymore."

That night, twelve people were delivered from suicidal and self-destructive thoughts and tendencies! Because I distinguished between my own thoughts and the accuser's voice *and* used my authority to silence the villain, heaven's thoughts overtook the ones from hell, not only for me but also for a dozen other people who had no idea what had happened that afternoon.

God had a purpose for all thirteen of us. Even before He said, *"Let there be light"* (Genesis 1:3), He made plans for us. Ephesians 1:4 says, *"He chose us in him **before the creation of the world** to be holy and blameless in his sight."* This is a sweet corollary to the promise that says, *"I know the plans I have for you,…plans to prosper you and not to harm you, plans to give you hope and a future"* (Jeremiah 29:11). God's plans are eternal.

Your spirit was in Him before He created the universe. Has someone told you that your birth was an accident? It wasn't. Even if you were the product of an "unplanned pregnancy"—even if you don't know your birth parents—you were no accident. God already knew you; then, at the right time, He knit you together in your mother's womb. (See Psalm 139:13.)

Before mankind fell (or even existed), God's plan to redeem you—spirit, soul, and body—was in place. Scripture says that Christ is *"the Lamb who was slain from the creation of the world"* (Revelation 13:8).

This is a mystery to our natural minds, but it is true! Our Savior bore the issues of our souls on the cross and was satisfied in knowing that His suffering restored us. (See Isaiah 53:11.) He paid a great price because there is great power in a soul that has been redeemed.

Like Father, like Child

God created you in His image and likeness. (See Genesis 1:26–27.) He is triune: Father, Son, and Holy Spirit. Therefore, you, too, have three parts: spirit, soul, and, body. As we discussed earlier, the soul has three parts, as well: mind, will, and emotions. Your mind is your intellect. Your will is the dreaming part of you, or your imagination. Your emotions involve your conscience, which governs your interactions and relational boundaries and enables you to feel such things as guilt and joy.

Before he sinned, Adam saw what God saw and spoke what God spoke. Adam's mind was not preoccupied with self but with God, as well as with Eve and with the rest of God's creation. Adam perceived God's intentions and spoke them out. That's how he named the animals. The power of the human soul was phenomenal! But when Adam and Eve blew it, the functioning of their souls was impaired.

Has your "soul functioning" ever broken down? Mine has. Life seems to move so quickly that my brain doesn't always keep up. One day, I left my wallet at the supermarket checkout. Six hours later, as my head hit my pillow, I "saw" my wallet. I jumped out of bed and rushed to the store before closing time. Thankfully, my wallet was waiting there, with my cash and credit cards intact. As a precaution, I canceled my cards and ordered new ones. The next day, I forgot about it and tried to use a canceled card.

The cashier said, "Your card has been rejected."

Ouch. I smiled and said, "I'm sorry. Can you hold on to my stuff? I'll be right back!"

The faces people make during such moments can tempt you to be defensive about nothing. My old card was dead, and my new card was waiting to be activated. There was nothing wrong with my purchasing power and nothing scurrilous about my identity. I just needed to use the right card.

There is a parallel here to the finished work of the cross. Jesus has already redeemed our souls. All we have to do is accept the sacrifice and walk in it. Paul said it this way: *"May God himself, the God of peace, sanctify you through and through. May your whole spirit, soul and body be kept blameless at the coming of our Lord Jesus Christ"* (1 Thessalonians 5:23).

The Greek word translated *"be kept"* means "to be looked at and guarded from loss or injury."[1] The good news is that God promises to guard our whole being—spirit, soul, and body—from loss and injury, as well as to help it grow to maturity. That's enough to make me want to do a "happy dance," but the redeemed soul and the restored imagination do more than just fuel our feelings—they are the connection between our spiritual engine and our heavenly destination.

What a Redeemed Imagination Can Accomplish

When we harness the power of the redeemed imagination and set our hearts on things above, heavenly things happen. The Old Testament prophet Isaiah had not been redeemed by the work of Christ, but he tasted heaven when he was commissioned by God:

In the year that King Uzziah died, I saw the Lord, high and exalted, seated on a throne; and the train of his robe filled the temple. Above him were seraphim, each with six wings: With two wings they covered their faces, with two they covered their feet, and with two they were flying. And they were calling to one another: "Holy, holy, holy is the Lord Almighty; the whole earth is full of his glory." At the sound of their voices the doorposts and thresholds shook and the temple was filled with smoke. (Isaiah 6:1–4)

In the atmosphere of God's glory, Isaiah's brokenness became plain. He cried, *"Woe to me!…I am ruined! For I am a man of unclean lips, and I live among a people of unclean lips, and my eyes have seen the King, the Lord Almighty"* (Isaiah 6:5). Yet God's purpose was not to crush Isaiah but to transform him. Isaiah continued,

Then one of the seraphim flew to me with a live coal in his hand, which he had taken with tongs from the altar. With it he touched my mouth

and said, "See, this has touched your lips; your guilt is taken away and your sin atoned for." (Isaiah 6:6–7)

Immediately, God called Isaiah, and he accepted the call. (See Isaiah 6:8.) He was not the first man to see heavenly realms. Moses saw them when he was up on the mountain in the cloud with God. Moses also was called to bring the scene to earth by building the tabernacle.

Long after Moses and Isaiah were gone from this earth, Peter, James, and John glimpsed the unseen realm when Jesus visited with Moses and Elijah in a cloud—again, atop a mountain. This time, the scene clarified God's purposes for the men. Peter, for one, needed the clarification! When he saw Jesus transfigured, his thoughts went to tabernacle-building. He said, "Lord, I will build three tabernacles—one for You, one for Moses, and one for Elijah."

It was a nice religious idea, but it was not God's idea. God said, "No, Peter. Let's not do that. Listen to My Son. He will tell you what to do."

Jesus told His disciples, "Don't reveal to anyone what you saw until after I am taken back to My Father in heaven." In other words, "Keep a lid on this until the Son of Man has been raised from the dead." (See, for example, Matthew 17:4–5, 9 kjv.)

The heavenly experience on the mountain gave Peter a lot to consider. In time, he would understand and write about it; but, by then, his thoughts would come from heaven. He would understand that we *may participate in the divine nature, having escaped the corruption in the world…* (2 Peter 1:4), and he would describe what that looked like (see 2 Peter 1:5–8). He would also explain the key to living like heaven: It is a matter of "refreshing our memory" in regard to God's truth for as long as we live in the tent (or *tabernacle*) of a physical body. (See 2 Peter 1:13.)

But, at the time of the transfiguration, the vow of silence that Jesus demanded of His disciples seemed strange. Why would He allow Himself to be seen in glory, only to ask those who had seen Him to keep it a secret? One reason is that God's intent could not be correctly understood by Peter and the other disciples at that time. Yet the heavenly experience became the seed for future heavenly thoughts.

God often lures us into experiences we don't understand so He can give us comprehension we have never had before. The transfiguration was one of those experiences for Peter.

Pastor Bill Johnson is a "heaven thinker." He explains (as we also saw in chapter 4) that the Greek word used for the transformation of Jesus' physical body into pure light is the same word used by Paul in urging us to *"be **transformed** by the renewing of* [our] *mind"* (Romans 12:2).[2]

The transfiguration experience had a purpose, but repeating the instructions God had already given Moses for a tabernacle was not it. God did not desire a new earthly (material) house to live in. Nor did He want to erect tabernacles for saints who were in heaven. Only after Jesus was resurrected did Peter realize that God wanted to make him and James and John (as well as us and all believers!) into tabernacles that would carry heaven down into the valleys of life.

This is exactly what happened when Jesus came down the mountain. He confronted a chaotic scene—a crowd ranting and a father weeping because the disciples who had remained in the valley had failed to heal the father's epileptic son. (See, for example, Matthew 17:14–16.)

I often wonder what the scene looked like. These nine guys had been walking and talking with Jesus daily, yet they had failed to get supernatural results. No doubt, if Peter had been there instead of up on the mountain, he would have given the boy's healing a shot. In his "If Jesus can do it, I can do it" manner, he might have copied a Jesus technique—like spitting in the boy's eye. (See, for example, Mark 8:22–26.) James and John, the *"sons of thunder"* (Mark 3:17), might have taken a supernatural tag-team wrestling approach to beat the demon out of the kid. Thomas would have stood back, shaking his head and saying, "I doubt that will work." And Judas? He would have suggested that taking up a large offering could get the boy healed.

I admit it—none of those scenarios is actually in the Bible. But we do know that nothing the disciples did worked. So, after Jesus set the boy free, His disciples asked Him, "Why couldn't we heal the boy? What did we do wrong?" (See, for example, Matthew 17:19.)

Jesus had already used the words *"unbelieving and perverse"* (Matthew 17:17) in His response to those who were at the scene. The language is strong, but Jesus was not addressing the disciples' actions. He was addressing their thinking. The word *"unbelieving"* suggests a person who has ample evidence yet refuses to be convinced. The word *"perverse"* indicates someone who distorts or misinterprets.[3] In very direct Jesus-talk, the Messiah told them, in effect, "You didn't do anything wrong; you were *thinking* wrong."

Jesus knew that their thinking would eventually straighten out, because He knew what God planned to do. He would send His Spirit to live in them, and they would be His temple, seated with Christ in heavenly places! Once Jesus ascended to heaven, their imaginations would be restored to "factory settings," and they would embrace their assignments.

They would change their world—and we would change ours.

A Ministry "Redeemed"

I once heard about an itinerant gospel musician named Matt who loved bow hunting. He and his wife traveled and ministered together, "but it was hard to make ends meet. With a young son at home and a second on the way, Matt looked for guidance."[4]

Matt prayed for a way to continue in ministry without worrying about money. The answer would come in stages, over several years, but, initially, his prayer was answered in the middle of the night, when he awoke with an idea for a new hunting bow. He describes the experience, saying, "It was just like there was a sheet of paper in front of my face."[5] Mathews, Inc., bows are now the standard in the industry! God used Matt McPherson's redeemed imagination to fulfill His purposes and to meet a family's needs.

Where a Redeemed Imagination Can Go

Have you ever heard something in your heart that sounded weird? I'm not talking about the accuser's voice; I'm talking about hearing from heaven. I recently had a conversation with a very intelligent individual who is a professor and holds multiple doctorates. During our conversation, she asked, "Can you tell me something that God wants me to know?"

I'm not God or a Ph.D., so I said, "I can't tell you anything, but I will ask God whether He will." As I began to pray, I saw a picture with an unusual word. I said, "I see God opening a door for you into a community that is *cloistered*."

Cloistered was practically a foreign word to me. I said it only because it was written over the door God showed me. The woman immediately affirmed the idea. She said, "Yes, that's exactly right. I visited a cloistered community yesterday."

I thought, *Are you kidding me?*

She explained that she and her colleagues were studying a mystic community, and there was a plaque over the entrance to the place that read Cloistered.

As confident as I can be, I am not always positive about what I see and hear. So, if it turns out not to be God, I am humble enough to apologize to people. If it is Him, I am humble enough to receive whatever input they give me. In this case, the word was exactly right, which was encouraging to the professor and to me.

Your redeemed imagination will take you places you don't fully understand. Don't let uncertainty keep you from responding to what God wants to do. Do your best, and if you get it wrong, admit it. To serve Him, you have to be willing to take risks. Just trust Him.

The Redeemed Imagination and Culture

God said, "*My thoughts are not your thoughts, neither are your ways my ways*" (Isaiah 55:8). We need to bear this truth in mind when the world's ways drive us to distraction. We want to believe that if everyone would "do the right thing," the world would be great. But the real issue isn't what people *do*. It's how they *think*. Society will change when hearts change. Even changing the laws won't transform how people think. They need to receive God's thoughts, and so do we. That is how culture is transformed.

Do you remember what happened when Peter saw his "lobster and bacon" vision in Acts 10? God turned his thinking about food and about Gentiles inside out. God is still doing things like that today. I have a friend who works in a country where people believe that pork corrodes your insides and ultimately kills you.

Someone asked him, "Are you a Christian? Do you eat bacon?"

He thought, *Oh, no. I'm dead.* It was forbidden in that country to share your Christian faith. The question could easily have been a trap.

The person who asked about the bacon continued, "I was told that if I ate bacon, worms would eat my insides out. Then my friends played a joke on me. They sneaked bacon onto my cheeseburger, and nothing happened, except that it tasted amazing. Now I want to know whether I've been believing lies all this time, because if bacon is this good, what else am I missing out on?"

God opened a *"great door for effective work"* (1 Corinthians 16:9), and my friend walked through it. Because this fellow had asked a question about bacon, my friend was able to share the gospel—and who knows how far that will go! Prior to Peter's vision, every Christian was a Jew. Two thousand years later, there are millions of Christians who are not Jewish. Why? Because thinking changed, and it affected the culture. Today, many Jewish people do know Jesus as Messiah, although many still do not. I believe a similar change in thinking is coming, so that the number of Jewish believers will rise in the days ahead. God can change any person's mind—anywhere, anytime—and the transformation can affect entire nations.

The Redeemed Conscience

Adam and Eve first hid from God when their consciences, which had been created clean, were stained. The human conscience had allowed them to feel emotions, such as joy, and to commune with God, but now it caused them to flee His presence. Jesus redeemed the conscience so we could return to the pure fellowship that God desires to share with us. The redeemed are confident before God. That is what He wants—for us to be comfortable around Him.

The book of Hebrews says that Jesus' blood *"cleanse*[s] *our consciences from acts that lead to death"* (Hebrews 9:14). Our spiritual senses of seeing, hearing, and feeling come through the conscience, where we experience both guilt and conviction. Guilt comes from the fallen nature. You'll remember that guilt keeps us bound to the past. Conviction is different from guilt. It comes from the redeemed conscience, and it tells us when we are missing the mark. We should not fear feeling convicted, because it is a manifestation of God's goodness that leads us to change our minds and our actions. (See Romans 2:4 NKJV, KJV.)

This is conviction's critical mission. It urges us to turn away from sin and to turn toward God. Repeatedly ignoring the conviction of the Holy Spirit sears the conscience and hardens the heart. A childhood experience helped me to understand how that works.

Growing up, I liked saving stuff. When I got candy for Christmas or Easter, I would save it and sell it to my siblings months later. I had a fairly successful racket! It was fun making and saving money. And when my piggy bank was full, my friends and I would go to the convenience store up the road from my house to buy penny candy.

To us, it was as good as finding a pot of gold. There was a whole row of sweets selling for a penny apiece, including Bazooka bubble gum. One day, a friend dared me to stuff some Bazooka in my pocket and walk out. My strong conviction about doing right was outmatched by my competitive nature. I could not resist the dare. So, I stole six pieces of bubble gum.

On the way home, I stuffed all six pieces in my mouth. It was fun at first, but the farther I walked, the worse I felt. I tried acting like nothing was wrong, but conviction got the better of me. By the time I was halfway home, I told my friends I'd forgotten something at the store and needed to go back.

One friend asked, "What did you forget?"

"I've just got to go back." That was all I said as I turned around and walked away.

Six cents might not have mattered much to the store owner, but if I had ignored the conviction I felt, I would eventually have reasoned it away. That is how a seared conscience works. We find ways to deny legitimate guilt. We tell ourselves, "It's only six cents. The gum was stale anyhow."

God gave us a conscience so that we *would* feel conviction and other things. The redeemed conscience is too precious to sear. Jesus died to remove our stony hearts and to give us hearts of flesh—*His heart.* (See, for example, Ezekiel 11:19.)

Faith, Hope, and Love

A restored conscience knows God's heart and feels what He feels. Both are keys to walking in the supernatural. Faith, hope, and love are involved with the redeemed soul. We need to understand the connections.

Scripture says, *"These three remain: faith, hope and love. But the greatest of these is love"* (1 Corinthians 13:13). Let's see how these essentials work together, starting with love, since it is the greatest of the three. Love accesses God's heart. After all, God *is* love, right? (See 1 John 4:8, 16.) Love also opens the door to hope (how can we see God's heart and *not* be hopeful?), which allows us to understand His intentions. When we understand His plan, we have faith to accomplish it.

Take a moment for that to soak in. Now see how faith, hope, and love work with the redeemed soul: Love is the power source of a redeemed conscience. The redeemed conscience restores our ability to commune with God so we can identify with what He feels and do what He asks. Hope is the power source of the redeemed imagination that allows us to see the unseen. How can we function in supernatural dimensions without seeing the unseen? (As Paul wrote, hope that is seen is not really hope at all. [See Romans 8:24.]) Third, *"faith is the substance of things hoped for, the evidence of things not seen"* (Hebrews 11:1 NKJV, KJV). Faith brings the unseen into manifestation in the realm of the seen.

Love is the power to feel what God feels. Hope is the ability to see heavenly realms. Faith is the power to bring heaven to earth. Still, the greatest of these is love. Everything we do starts there, in the heart of God. This is true in regard to all things, including the prophetic. Notice what happened when Isaiah was given a troubling vision for Israel's enemies, Elam and Media:

> *A dire vision has been shown to me: The traitor betrays, the looter takes loot. Elam, attack! Media, lay siege! I will bring to an end all the groaning she caused. At this my body is racked with pain, pangs seize me, like those of a woman in labor; I am staggered by what I hear, I am bewildered by what I see.* (Isaiah 21:2–3)

Remember that our spiritual senses come through the conscience. Isaiah felt what God felt. His senses were triggered by God's message; he experienced pain and was bewildered by what he saw. Physically sensing God's message helped Isaiah to understand the importance of what God was saying.

A word of caution here: When our senses are triggered by prophetic experiences, we remain in charge of what we feel. Feelings are *not* in charge of us. Sometimes, in intercession, for example, you can feel the atmosphere of a place. You are not called to stay in the atmosphere you are sensing. The feeling serves a purpose, but true intercession isn't just feeling the atmosphere—it is *changing* the atmosphere. God put us on the earth to change the culture, not to become it.

Because our spiritual senses filter through the conscience, having a clear conscience is critical. Without it, our feelings get mixed up, and we misunderstand God's heart. For example, if I believe God is mad at me, I will likely project "His anger" toward other people, believing that it is *from* God. This is wrong. God is not mad at the world, and unless I believe God loves me, I cannot walk in His love toward others. Finally, unless I *believe* I am reconciled to God, I cannot minister reconciliation to others. (See 2 Corinthians 5:18.)

On the other hand, if I am wrapped in the love of Christ, I will see myself and others as He does. Paul explained,

> *Christ's love compels us, because we are convinced that one died for all, and therefore all died. And he died for all, that those who live should no*

longer live for themselves but for him who died for them and was raised again. So from now on we regard no one from a worldly point of view. Though we once regarded Christ in this way, we do so no longer. **Therefore, if anyone is in Christ, the new creation has come: The old has gone, the new is here! All this is from God, who reconciled us to himself through Christ and gave us the ministry of reconciliation:** *that God was reconciling the world to himself in Christ, not counting people's sins against them. And he has committed to us the message of reconciliation.*   (2 Corinthians 5:14–19)

What a powerful passage! When Christ died, I died with Him, along with my guilt and shame. I am raised with Him, too, but I no longer live for myself. Now I live for Christ, and I see with His eyes. If He doesn't count people's sins against them, I don't do it, either. (See, for example, John 5:19.)

When something is reconciled, it means that it "adds up" in relation to something else. One of the definitions of *reconcile* in *Merriam-Webster's* dictionary is "to check (a financial account) against another for accuracy."[6] Through Jesus, God made people "add up" to what He says about them. *Christ reconciled them to Himself.* He took their punishment so that they could be in relationship with God. He is not looking to judge them or to condemn them. He wants only to save them.

He loves the world. And we are His ambassadors!

David's Conscience Cried Out

David's adultery with Bathsheba was freighted with consequences. He arranged for the murder of Bathsheba's husband in order to cover his tracks. Then the child conceived in adultery died. David wrestled with his conscience and was confronted by the prophet Nathan. David later cried out to God, *"Create in me a pure heart, O God, and renew a steadfast spirit within me. Do not cast me from your presence or take your Holy Spirit from me. Restore to me the joy of your* *salvation and grant me a willing spirit, to sustain me. **Then I will teach transgressors your ways, so that sinners will turn back to you*** (Psalm 51:10–13).

David faced his guilt squarely—not at first, but in time. He laid himself bare before God and left the encounter with something positive. What He found in God's heart was a ministry: to testify to other sinners and to lead them to His love.

God took David's *mess* and gave him a *message*.

The "Three C's" of a Redeemed Conscience

Communion, confidence, and clarity—these are three key features of a redeemed conscience. A quick summary of each will be an apt way to close our discussion of the restored soul.

Communion

Guilt caused us to withdraw from God. Jesus came to take our sin and to redeem the human conscience so we could commune with God freely. Hebrews 10:22 encourages us to draw near to God with sincere hearts. God is saying, "When your guilt is gone, your heart is an open book. Instead of running from Me, you run toward Me. You know that I love you. I'm not angry with you, and you know I never will be. Your heart is tender and knows My heart."

Confidence

A redeemed conscience promotes confidence in approaching other people and the affairs of life. When guilt is out of the picture, blame is, too. We don't need to blame others for our mistakes or struggles because we know God is not looking to blame us or anyone else for mistakes and wrongdoing. *"God did not send his Son into the world to condemn the world, but to save the world through him"* (John 3:17). God's loving intentions for the world free us to love others and to function with confidence.

Clarity

Spiritual impressions, sights, and sounds are filtered through the conscience. Therefore, the condition of the conscience shapes spiritual perception. That is why Adam and Eve, who once enjoyed a blissful relationship with God, suddenly hid from Him. Their ability to think like heaven was compromised. The sound of God walking in the garden no longer brought them joy. (See Genesis 3:8.) Fear and shame impeded their ability to see and hear clearly. God's heart seemed hidden from them, and the future no longer appeared secure.

The mysteries of God are also filtered through the conscience. Paul understood clearly that he had been entrusted with mysteries that God had revealed. Paul had no problem telling others to regard him in this way. He did not fear being judged or criticized. His conscience was clear and allowed him to perceive and to act with clarity:

> This, then, is how you ought to regard us: as servants of Christ and as those entrusted with the mysteries God has revealed. Now it is required that those who have been given a trust must prove faithful. I care very little if I am judged by you or by any human court; indeed, I do not even judge myself. My conscience is clear, but that does not make me innocent. It is the Lord who judges me. Therefore judge nothing before the appointed time; wait until the Lord comes. He will bring to light what is hidden in darkness and will expose the motives of the heart.
>
> (1 Corinthians 4:1–5)

In the *New King James Version*, verse 4 reads differently: *"I know of nothing against myself, yet I am not justified by this; but He who judges me is the Lord."* The Greek word for *"know"* in this verse is *synoraō* or *suneidon*. Among its meanings are "to understand, perceive, comprehend" and "to know in one's mind or with one's self, to be conscious of."[7] This is the supernatural clarity Christ died to give us!

Jesus Christ redeemed our souls. He liberated us from guilt, fear, and shame. When we embrace His redemption, our ways are reconciled to His ways, and our hearts are reconciled to His heart. We feel what He feels and want what He wants. God desires to entrust us with His mysteries, just as

He did for Paul. A clear conscience allows us to come out of hiding and to walk free of critical self-judgment, as well as of negative judgments against others. When we have that kind of communion and clarity, we can see the things that are hidden for us in heaven.

When we think like heaven, we bring heaven to earth!

Thinking like Heaven

1. Ask God to show you how being *"kept blameless"* (in the sense of being able to see God's intentions clearly) affects a difficult area in your life. Write down what He reveals and ask Him how to walk it out.

2. Have you ever been skeptical about hearing God's voice? Have you heard something (such as a word of instruction, assurance, or guidance) and said, "That can't be Him"? Ask God to give you an example of when you may have done this, and to reveal the root of your skepticism. Then, ask Him to help you to become more discerning in recognizing His voice.

3. Ask God to give you a picture of your assignment as His ambassador. What is He showing you? How does it confirm and/or change your approach to the ministry of reconciliation?

4. Ask God to reveal areas where you are motivated by guilt and where you provoke others by using guilt against them. Evaluate your level of confidence (a key feature of a redeemed conscience) in those areas. Where you are living under guilt, accept your full redemption and forgiveness through Christ. Then, ask Him to show you how to be motivated by love, and how to motivate others by love, remembering that God's loving intentions for the world free us to love others and to function with confidence.

5. Take five to ten minutes each morning for personal communion with God. Be creative and thank Him for restoring your soul and for clearing your conscience of guilt and shame.

Notes

1. See electronic version of *Strong's Talking Greek & Hebrew Dictionary*, G5083, tēreō, QuickVerse 10, © WORDsearch, a division of LifeWay Christian Resources. All rights reserved.

2. Bill Johnson, *The Supernatural Power of a Transformed Mind* (Shippensburg, PA: Destiny Image Publishers, Inc., 2005), 42.

3. *Biblesoft's New Exhaustive Strong's Numbers and Concordance*, s.v. "diastrepho" (NT 1294).

4. Tim Dehn, "Inside the Mind of Matt McPherson," *ArrowTrade*, May 1997, http://c715222.r22.cf2.rackcdn.com/content/uploads/timeline/1998-May_97_ArrowTrade_Mathews_Profile.pdf.

5. Ibid.

6. *Merriam-Webster's 11ᵗʰ Collegiate Dictionary*, electronic version, © 2003, s.v. "reconcile."

7. Blue Letter Bible, Greek Lexicon, s.v. "synoraō" (*Strong's* NT 4894), https://www.blueletterbible.org/lang/lexicon/lexicon.cfm?Strongs=G4894&t=KJV.

7

The Supernatural Power of Love

Bob Hazlett @bob_hazlett
The world's love is reciprocal: "I love you, you love me…." God's love is redemptive: "God so loved the world that He gave." Period. #ThinklikeHeaven #LovelikeHeaven

↩   ↻   ★   •••

To get a fire going, one spark is all you need. Ask me how I know.

When I was a young boy, a neighbor friend and I became overly curious about a small pile of pine needles. We wondered how long it would take to ignite the pile with a single match. We soon learned that we could do it in no time flat. Thanks to our local fire department, the only damage and injury caused by the inferno were to a grove of mature pine trees. And thanks to the "heat" applied to my bottom by my dad, I never played with matches again.

Not all fires are bad, as the apostle Paul explained to his protégé Timothy.

*I am reminded of your sincere faith, which first lived in your grand-mother Lois and in your mother Eunice and, I am persuaded, now lives in you also. For this reason I remind you to **fan into flame the*** *gift of God, which is in you through the laying on of my hands. For the Spirit God gave us does not make us timid, but gives us power, love and self-discipline.* (2 Timothy 1:5–7)

The gift of God is given by Him but must be fanned into flame by us. I vividly remember a spark God dropped into my life when I was a teen. I have been fanning it ever since. It began as I read these verses in Romans:

For I am convinced that neither death nor life, neither angels nor demons, neither the present nor the future, nor any powers, neither height nor depth, nor anything else in all creation, will be able to separate us from the love of God that is in Christ Jesus our Lord. (Romans 8:38–39)

I wept over those words as God burned away some things and lit something new in me. The insecurity of a religious, performance-based relationship with God went up in smoke; but the flame of His love burned red-hot, and still does.

Keep the Flame Burning

There is a powerful yet funny moment in the movie *Cast Away*. Tom Hanks plays Chuck Noland, a FedEx executive who survives a plane crash and ends up alone on a deserted island. When Noland creates fire, he knows he has found a key to his survival. He celebrates his relief, joy, and renewed confidence by dancing around on the beach. He is still a castaway. He is still far from home. But in his grim circumstances, he finds one spark and fans it into a raging fire.[1]

When Paul told Timothy to fan into flame his gift, he explained why: *"For God has not given us a spirit of fear, but of power and of love and of a sound mind"* (2 Timothy 1:7 NKJV). Fear is a wet blanket that snuffs out the spiritual flame we are supposed to cultivate. The God who gave us supernatural gifts did not send a spirit of fear to tamp them down. He enabled us to overcome fear and to burn brightly for Him.

My wife, Kim, has a musical gift. Don't ask me how it works, but her gift comes through her keyboard. I know the thing is made of circuits and plastic parts, yet when the notes pass through the sound system and hit my eardrums, I hear *Kimberly*. As she plays, an atmosphere is created. Whatever the song or the key, Kimberly comes through it.

The same thing happens when you use your gifts. Maybe yours involves words. When you speak, you bring the light of God's presence into the chaos around you. Whatever your language, your voice becomes the sound of *"Christ in you, the hope of glory"* (Colossians 1:27). That is what people hear—His gift working in and through you.

You cannot create your gifts; they come from God and work supernaturally. Yet you have to fan the flame. No one can do it for you. You must do it yourself. The more you do, the more you grow spiritually. And if you don't, you risk extinguishing those gifts.

That is not what God planned! Do you remember when we talked about being *"kept blameless"* (1 Thessalonians 5:23)? The context of the promise is a warning not to tamp down the supernatural workings of God:

> *Do not quench the Spirit. Do not treat prophecies with contempt but test them all; hold on to what is good, reject every kind of evil. May God himself, the God of peace, sanctify you through and through. May your whole spirit, soul and body be kept blameless at the coming of our Lord Jesus Christ.* (1 Thessalonians 5:19–23)

The Holy Spirit and the supernatural are inseparable. You cannot quench one and experience the other. Don't be a wet blanket, smothering your gifts. Fan your flame!

Love and Fire Are Connected

Remember what Paul said in 1 Corinthians 13:13: *"Now these three remain: faith, hope and love. But the greatest of these is love."* In the very next verse, he said, *"Follow the way of love and eagerly desire gifts of the Spirit, especially prophecy"* (1 Corinthians 14:1). Did you notice how Paul linked love with the operation of spiritual gifts? Don't be distracted by the chapter break; Paul didn't write his epistles with chapter numbers. Nor did he think love would be a nice "add-on."

We have turned 1 Corinthians 13 into a Hallmark card about love, but Paul linked it—in unbroken context—with the supernatural. He combined the topics of love and spiritual gifts because they are inseparable. Prophecy and other gifts involve seeing people and situations through the heart of God's love. These gifts are not just about having the mind of Christ; they are also about having the heart of Christ *for people*. All the gifts are designed to operate through love.

Earlier in chapter 13, Paul made another critical point about love and the gifts:

> *Love never fails. But whether there are prophecies, they will fail; whether there are tongues, they will cease; whether there is knowledge, it will vanish away. For we know in part and we prophesy in part. But when that which is perfect has come, then that which is in part will be done away.* (1 Corinthians 13:8–10 NKJV)

A lot of people read this passage and say, "See! There's the proof that prophecy has disappeared." But Paul was not talking about prophecy. He was talking about perfect love. When love is complete, the perfect has come. When we are perfected in love, we see as God sees. Our vision is not obscured or immature but perfected.

> *When I was a child, I spoke as a child, I understood as a child, I thought as a child; but when I became a man, I put away childish things. For now we see in a mirror, dimly, but then face to face. Now I know in part, but then I shall know just as I also am known. And now abide faith, hope, love, these three; but the greatest of these is love.* (1 Corinthians 13:11–13 NKJV)

Love keeps us tuned to God's ways of seeing and doing. It fans the flame and keeps our fires burning. Our physical strength might ebb and flow, but *"love never fails"* (1 Corinthians 13:8 NKJV).

Not long ago, I ministered in South America at a large conference of several thousand young people. At meetings this large, I don't have the same opportunities for personal ministry that I relish at smaller events.

For this conference, we trained a team of about 125 young people to serve those who requested prayer and other ministry.

My conference schedule was tightly packed. However, one afternoon, a man asked me, "Would you pray for some of the leaders? They are waiting in a room off to the side."

"Sure," I said. "How many leaders are there?"

The man said, "There are twelve…maybe fifteen…I guess about twenty."

I chuckled and thought, *The number is getting bigger and bigger, but OK.* Even if there were twenty-five or thirty people, we'd have enough time to pray for all of them.

The man led me to a little room where approximately thirty people were waiting. But a line had formed outside the room, and it kept growing! Before all was said and done, three-and-a-half hours had passed, and I had prayed and prophesied over 125 people in a room without air-conditioning or windows.

I had preached in the morning and was scheduled to preach again that night. The timing was tight, but the ministry was wonderful—just me, the Holy Spirit, and my interpreter. I loved it! God seriously touched people. Some wept, some laughed, and lots of hugs were exchanged. There was a continual "changing of the guard"; in order for a new group to enter the room, an earlier group had to leave. It was a slow process.

At one point, my interpreter asked me, "How do you keep going? How do you figure out what to say next? How do you have all this energy?"

Controlling all that was above my pay grade. I told him, "The Bible says there is a time when prophecy will cease, but love will never fail. So, I don't try to keep prophesying. I don't ask God for more prophecy or more energy. I just ask Him for more love, because if love never fails, I'll never run out of things that God wants to tell people."

That is part of what I believe Paul tried to convey to the church at Corinth. If you focus on operating in the spiritual gifts, you can fail. But if you focus on God's love, failure is impossible.

Jesus demonstrated this reality in His own life. Let's look at one example.

> He came to a town in Samaria called Sychar, near the plot of ground Jacob had given to his son Joseph. Jacob's well was there, and Jesus, **tired as he was from the journey**, sat down by the well. It was about noon. (John 4:5–6)

Jesus was so tired and hungry from ministry that His disciples left Him near a well in Samaria and went to get food. As He sat alone, a woman came to draw water. Jesus' heart of love perceived her need. She had been through multiple marriages and was living with yet another man. Jesus reached out to her and shared the gospel. She was so transformed by His supernatural ministry that she ran to get her neighbors, many of whom were evangelized that same day.

When the woman first arrived, the Messiah was weak from hunger and from the journey. But, in love, He fanned the flame and spoke prophetically to her. When Jesus' disciples returned with food, He was refreshed and satisfied. He said, in essence, "I don't need anything to eat; My food and My drink is to do the will of My Father in heaven." (See John 4:34.)

What a powerful statement that is! Jesus showed us that refreshing comes when we pour out God's love to people. He demonstrated why love never fails.

The Elements of Spiritual Fire

Now that we have seen the link between love and the supernatural, let's dig a little deeper into the workings of fire—both in the natural realm and in the supernatural realm. We know that in order to start and stoke a natural fire, we must have heat, fuel, and air (oxygen). If one of these elements is missing, fire is impossible.

Similarly, spiritual fire requires a combination of elements, but its three essential components are faith, hope, and love. We have already seen how faith, hope, and love work in the redeemed soul. And, previously in this chapter, we saw how love works in association with the spiritual gifts. Love keeps us thinking like heaven, where all things are possible. And love always produces good expectations, or *hope*. When I see with God's eyes of love, I perceive His optimism about your future, and I hear Him telling you, "I know the plan that I have for you, a plan to prosper you and not to harm you, to give you a future and a hope." (See Jeremiah 29:11.) If He gives me a word for you, it won't sound like a doomsday report!

The triad is complete when hope leads to faith. Once you and I have the same sense of expectancy that God does, faith provides the substance of whatever is hoped for (see Hebrews 11:1 NKJV, KJV), and the gifts lead to tangible results.

Do you see how faith, hope, and love help to keep the fire burning? Now hold that thought, because there is another "twist": I believe that faith, hope, and love are connected to the three items Paul mentioned to Timothy in 2 Timothy 1:7 (NKJV)—power, love, and a sound mind.

Notice that love is mentioned in each group of three. That makes sense, because *"the greatest of these is love"* (1 Corinthians 13:13). Now let's take power, love, and a sound mind in a different order: I understand God's heart in the context of His love, and it fans the flame within me. It also drives out fear, because God's love is perfect. (See 1 John 4:18.) Therefore, I have a sound mind and can see hope clearly. My thinking is not muddled due to anxiety and doubt; instead, my expectations match His. Now, power becomes my access to His faith, which is released to fulfill His purposes.

How *amazing* God's ways are!

When I shared these truths with a group in Dallas, Texas, a young man came to me after the lunch break very excited about the teaching. He talked to me about what God was revealing to him. The idea of perfect love driving out fear had gripped him. He was especially aware that when love is not the focus, we fear people who are different from us.

He said, "I thought about the people I'm most afraid of."

His words took me by surprise. He was a big guy and looked pretty tough. I wondered, *How can he be afraid of anyone? Plus, he's got a million-dollar smile. Who would see him and not love him right off the bat?*

So I asked, "Who are you afraid of?"

He said, "Old people." It was the last thing I expected to hear.

He explained, "Old people scare me. Whenever I got in trouble as a kid, my grandmother pulled me by the ear. She loved us, but she could be tough. Old people just scare me sometimes."

"What are you doing with that?" I asked.

"I went to Walmart," he said, "because I figured there would be lots of old people there."

What a God-idea! Starting with the greeters, he found older people to pray for. He said, "It was great. One lady had a cane, and God healed her. She didn't pull my ear, but she pinched my cheeks. It was awesome!"

He hadn't really been afraid of old people but of people who were different from him. Through this situation, God revealed an area in which he was not yet perfected in love. But when he went on his mission to Walmart, he overcame the intimidation.

I gave him a high five and thanked him for sharing his story. The next morning, he looked downcast, saying, "Man, I need you to pray for me."

"Why?"

"Because I'm just not getting this love thing."

I asked what had happened, and he told me, "Driving home last night, I stopped at an intersection, and a prostitute walked in front of my car. I immediately felt the compassion of God. I was like, 'Man, I want to pray for her. I want her to know who God created her to be.'"

Just as he had been about to pray for the prostitute, he realized that "she" was a he. The idea of a transvestite prostitute was intimidating to him. Instead of wanting to help, he had felt angry. *What is this guy doing?* he had wondered.

The young man told me, "I didn't want to help anymore. So, I left. I didn't feel any love, and it frustrated me because I thought I was growing in love."

He had left the scene more upset with himself than with the transvestite. The devil had worked him over with condemnation, which is why he had said, "I'm just not getting this love thing."

I replied, "Put your hand up and give me a high five."

When I high-fived him, he asked, "Why are you doing that?"

"Because you are growing in love."

"What do you mean?"

I said, "Last week, you probably would have stopped at the same intersection, done nothing, and left without feeling a thing. You would have thought your anger and disdain were righteous, right?"

My hypothesis wasn't exactly right, but it was close. Something had changed in him. Love was showing him where he needed to grow. The fact that he still felt fearful was a signal. It said that more growth was coming.

When that happens to me, I say, "God, thank You for helping me to grow in love." The fact that I recognize my own feelings of intimidation tells me that I can get past them. When I embrace God's love for me, I can embrace His love for others. And love never fails.

Courage from a Nurturing God

Courage does not grow on trees, but it can be developed. We have already seen that love drives out fear and that *the one who fears is not made perfect in love* (1 John 4:18). God's love is the ultimate source of courage. His love nurtures us, and our courage grows! The process is replicated in nature, as I discovered while reading about scientists who study fear and courage. Some researchers are even working to develop a "courage pill" to help people cope with anxiety disorders, stress, and inordinate fears of spiders, snakes, and the like.[2]

Some research involves those who serve in the United States Army Special Forces. Studies have shown that these warriors respond differently to danger than most people do. Instead of becoming fearful and panicky, they become laser-focused. When under pressure, their bodies produce less of the stress hormone cortisol and more neuropeptide Y, which improves performance under stress.[3]

Since these men's brains obviously cannot be dissected, rats' brains have been studied. Scientists bred rodents into two groups: one consisting of those that were very fearful, and one made up of those that became very focused in dangerous situations. When they autopsied the rats, they discovered that the amygdala (a part of the brain connected to fear and courage) of the courageous rats had receptors able to accept proteins that produce a calming effect.

Fear and Courage

Perfect love drives out fear! It's hard to be afraid of what you love, and it's difficult to love what you are afraid of.

The fearful rats lacked these receptors, so scientists wondered whether it was possible to change that. They put the "scaredy-rats" under the care of rodent mothers that had previously raised courageous offspring. These mothers behaved differently than the natural mothers of the fearful rats. The foster mothers stayed very close and even slept on top of their new "kids." Gradually, the behavior of the fearful rats changed, and they began taking risks. When their brains were examined, they had grown the receptors they had previously lacked!

Much work has been done to demonstrate the effects of maternal presence and nurturing in reducing fear responses.[4] I cannot help but think about King David, who was apparently born without the care and love of his father, was forsaken by his family, and was left alone with the flocks. When the prophet Samuel came to anoint the next king, David's father, Jesse, presented to him seven sons, none of whom won the Lord's approval. Samuel realized there had to be another son, so he asked, "Do you have another son I don't know about?" (See 1 Samuel 16:1–13.)

Jesse said, "Oh yeah, I forgot. I have another son. He's out with the flocks."

You forgot your eighth son? *Really?*

Jesse had had no intention of presenting David. As far as he was concerned, the words *David* and *king* did not belong in the same sentence. Even knowing that the great prophet was on a divine assignment, Jesse discounted the one son whom God had chosen!

We can see from this story that David was not naturally aggressive. He certainly did not push his way into the king-selecting ceremony. Yet something happened when he was anointed by Samuel. David now had a promise from God. It came with its share of problems, but even the problems would serve God's greater purpose of making David a strong king. So, when lions and bears came to attack the family's flock, David responded as a fierce warrior would. He did not defend a kingdom but rather some sheep belonging to the father who cared not a whit about him.

By the time David offered to take down Goliath, he was as bold as a lion. His conversation with King Saul reveals a young man with a very courageous heart.

> *Saul replied, "You are not able to go out against this Philistine and fight him; you are only a young man, and he has been a warrior from his youth." But David said to Saul, "Your servant has been keeping his father's sheep. When a lion or a bear came and carried off a sheep from the flock, I went after it, struck it and rescued the sheep from its mouth. When it turned on me, I seized it by its hair, struck it and killed it. Your servant has killed both the lion and the bear; this uncircumcised Philistine will be like one of them, because he has defied the armies of the living God. The LORD who rescued me from the paw of the lion and the paw of the bear will rescue me from the hand of this Philistine."*
>
> (1 Samuel 17:33–37)

You don't need a pill to make you courageous. You just need to know you have a Father who loves you and has your back. God is a nurturer—Father and Mother in one. He cares about you. He covers you. He uplifts you. His nurturing ways can turn you into a fearless warrior who runs toward the battle with joy. Then, "old people" won't scare you. People who are confused about their gender and identity won't scare you, either. Those who define themselves by their idols and by the culture around them will find that you don't use these things as yardsticks. Instead, you see God's definition of them. You therefore accept and love them as they are—and you treat them as the people they are destined to become.

Changing people is not our job; loving them is. Then God's love changes both them and us. Supernatural love is *powerful!*

Thinking like Heaven

1. What gift(s) has God given you? How does He (or how is He waiting to) use your gifts to shift atmospheres and to convey His love? Ask Him!

2. Have you experienced an "exhausted at the well" moment, as Jesus did? If so, how did you respond? If you see this moment differently now, explain in what way.

3. Ask God to reveal the faith-hope-love connection in regard to someone whom He has asked you to touch with the gospel. How will these "fire starters" affect your approach to this assignment? What role will power, love, and a sound mind play?

4. What kinds of situations or people do you tend to shy away from? Ask God to reveal the sources of your fears. Then ask Him for strategies to overcome them. And follow through!

5. How do you believe God wants to nurture you in His love? Ask Him to reveal what His nurturing looks like and how it will make you courageous in an area that tends to make you fearful.

Notes

1. *Cast Away*, released by Twentieth Century Fox Film Corporation, 2000; credits found at IMDb, "Cast Away," http://www.imdb.com/title/ ttUI6J2222/?rcf_=ttcc_co_ti

2. George Dvorsky, "Could a Single Pill Make You Fearless?" io9, *Mad Science* news, June 13, 2012, http://io9.com/5917936/could-a-single-pill-make-you-fearless.

3. Dr. C. A. Morgan III and Major Gary Hazlett, "Assessment of Humans Experiencing Uncontrollable Stress," *Special Warfare*, Summer 2000, U.S. Army John F. Kennedy Special Warfare Center and School, Fort Bragg, North Carolina.

4. See, for example, Regina Sullivan, Ph.D., and Elizabeth Norton Lasley, "Fear in Love: Attachment, Abuse, and the Developing Brain," *Cerebrum*, September 1, 2010, U.S. National Library of Medicine, National Institutes of Health, http://www.ncbi.nlm.nih.gov/pmc/articles/PMC3574772/, and Stephanie Moriceau and Regina M. Sullivan, "Maternal Presence Serves as a Switch Between Learning Fear and Attraction in Infancy," NIH Public Access Author Manuscript, U.S. National Library of Medicine, National Institutes of Health, July 9, 2006, http://www.ncbi.nlm.nih.gov/pmc/articles/PMC1560090/.

8

Permission to Step Up

Bob Hazlett @bob_hazlett
If you are experiencing a lot of opposition right now, you are already at the next level. Push-back comes whenever you are pushing forward! #ThinklikeHeaven #StepUp

Big families have lots of stuff. As one of five kids, I remember shoes of various sizes and colors being kicked off after school or play. They never put themselves away, so an angel named Mom moved them closer to their destination by collecting them and lining them up on the stairs. She thought we'd get the hint and take our shoes with us on the next trip up, but her plan backfired. The shoes became part of the scenery, and the stairs became the Hazlett Shoe Depot. At night, we walked past them on our way to bed; when morning came, we retrieved our respective pairs and headed out for school.

The Depot was fairly functional, at least until you ventured up or down the stairs in the dark. Then you had a fifty-fifty chance of breaking your neck or some other important body part. As you applied ice to the knot on your head, you realized that the Hazlett Shoe Depot was not a benign part of the landscape; it was an obstacle course that could keep you from reaching your destination in one piece.

Early on, we talked about how God prepares the next level for us. This includes "clearing the stairway," in the heavenly sense, so that we have an unobstructed passage to that next level. One of the ways we learn to think like heaven happens when we are not thinking—at least not consciously. Our minds usually seem most restful when we sleep, so sleep is a great time for heaven to invade earth through dreams. Dreaming is a function of the subconscious mind and the conscious mind alike. When we become aware of our dreams, we are not just spectators in them. We can become participants, as well.

Not long ago, I had such a dream. I stood on an ancient stairway leading to a door that many people had attempted to open but could not. I knew I had to get beyond the door to bring God's light and kingdom into that dark place. However, the steps were cluttered with "stuff" left behind by those whose efforts had failed. I began removing the clutter myself, but it was slow going. Then I heard a voice—it was the voice of a cleaning woman at the bottom of the stairs. She had bright white hair and the clearest blue eyes. She asked me a pointed question: "Are you ready for the next level?"

I knew from her tone that she was not asking me whether I had readied myself for that level. She was asking me whether I was ready to be taken there. Her question was not about preparation but about permission. I stood straight up, looked her in the eye, and said, "I am ready!"

Immediately, a cleaning crew appeared behind her, and each member of the crew looked just like her. She said, "Good, then we are here to get the next level ready for you."

With that, they began cleaning the stairway.

This dream was a parable for me, but it led to very practical results. During that time, I was involved in three major projects that had stalled, one of which was this book. Within three days of this dream, all three projects were back on track.

The dream's meaning is clear. Sometimes, while we are trying hard to prepare ourselves to reach the next level, God is simply asking our permission to take us there. The moment we say, "I am ready!" His heavenly cleaning crew makes the next level ready for us. *With heaven's invitation comes heaven's empowerment!*

Sometime after my dream, during corporate worship, God gave me a similar vision of a long stairway traveled by very few people and leading upward to various doors that had rarely been opened. Behind those doors were unusual places.

I asked the Lord, "What is that?"

He said, "That is the next level. It is an unfamiliar place to all but a few. I'm taking some people there now."

Permission granted. Are you ready to accept?

Perception, Proclamation, Permission

We are learning to think like heaven because there is someplace higher we must go. Heavenly thinking is the ticket. It is supernatural but practical. We need three elements in order to connect with that place: perception, proclamation, and permission. Let's check them out.

When God speaks, things happen. What better example is there than the Creation? God proclaimed, *"Let there be light"*—and light appeared. (See Genesis 1:3.) God's proclamation was preceded by His perception: *"The earth was formless and empty, darkness was over the surface of the deep"* (Genesis 1:2). God perceived the situation and spoke to it. His authority issued permission for worlds to be created, *"so that what is seen was not made out of what was visible"* (Hebrews 11:3).

This is a template for thinking like heaven! We learn to see as God sees, and we accurately proclaim His intent. We speak in His name (with His authority), issuing permission for transformation. When perplexed by the world's mixed-up ideas and unthinkable cruelty, we detect its cry for God's answer: *"For God so loved the world that he gave his one and only Son, that whoever believes in him shall not perish but have eternal life"* (John 3:16). We cannot help but proclaim the good news and activate a change for the better.

The same principle applies to hearing God speak. In this sense, permission is not a polite form of consent but a cutting-edge release. It happens when someone with authority perceives who you already are and releases you to become that and to do whatever that entails. It is like a father who realizes his daughter is ready to drive. He says, "Here you go, sweetheart" and hands her the car keys. He sees his "baby girl" driving, and he speaks words that facilitate that reality. Permission is granted.

What if the daughter misunderstood the conversation or thought her father was joking? What if her fear of driving by herself overrode her desire to be grown up? There are things we are not yet doing because we still have not recognized our readiness or have forgotten or distrusted our Father's permission. His permission has been granted, *but we are still waiting.*

Eternal Speak

God's words at the Creation of the world are producing even now. The light still shines, life still produces after its own kind, and the universe is still expanding. God's permission has not been revoked. To this day, the universe responds to His words.

Childhood Tears and Permission to Prophesy

Shoes weren't the only thing the Hazletts had lots of. We also had loads of books. Our "library" was a book pile in our hallway. Like anything else left in my reach, I dug into it. When I was about fourteen, I read Charles Finney's *Lectures on Revival*. By the time I graduated from high school, I'd read and reread five or so books about Smith Wigglesworth.

Another book captivated me. It was the story of T. L. Osborn, the American evangelist whose early experiences in India were disappointing to him. Discouraged, he came home and attended a William Branham meeting. Branham had words of knowledge for people and prayed for the sick. Osborn was deeply affected by Branham and implemented some ideas from Branham's ministry.

Osborn returned to India and became one of the great missionary evangelists of all time. I wept as I sat cross-legged in our hallway, reading his story and seeing pictures of large crowds being saved, healed, and set free. I did not realize it then, but the tears that fell onto the book's pages were tears of intercession, watering the seed of my future.

Decades later, a friend who had ministered for years in South America invited me to preach at the church he pastored in Miami. So, I preached and also prayed for people.

Afterward, he said, "Bob, you were prophesying to people."

"No I wasn't. I was praying for them."

He insisted, "No, you were prophesying."

"That's impossible. I couldn't have prophesied."

He asked, "Why not?"

My answer was circular but firm: "Because I don't believe in prophecy."

"Well then," he said, "you don't believe in yourself."

Boom! He had me. "What do you mean?"

"I mean you're a prophet," he said.

"No. I'm an evangelist."

"No you're not."

"Yes, I am. I have a plaque on my wall that says I'm an evangelist. And it's signed by some very important people." I was grasping at straws.

My friend said, "I want you to meet my pastor in South America. He's an apostle."

I said, "He can't be an apostle."

"Why not?"

"Because they don't exist."

"Well, yes, they do."

"What makes him an apostle?"

"Look, we have planted hundreds of churches down there."

"Well," I said, "I guess if there were such a thing as an apostle today, he would probably be doing stuff like that."

My friend won the round and took me to South America for an apostolic conference attended by leaders from all over South America and elsewhere—probably fifteen thousand people, all told. My friend and I sat in the second row. My Spanish was not good enough to keep up, so he interpreted for me.

At some point, he said, "Hey, they just mentioned you."

I thought he was messing with me, so I said, "Knock it off."

"I'm serious. He said that you're a prophet from America, and you came with a word for the nation."

"Shut up!" I said in disbelief.

My friend grabbed my arm. "We're going up right now. Do you have a word?"

"No!"

"Well, this would be a good time to get one."

The next thing I knew, I received a lengthy introduction, peppered with the word *profeta*, and was handed a microphone. I have no idea what I said, but it took ten or fifteen minutes to say it. *Hallelujahs* and *amens* rang out right and left as people ran to the front. It was a breakout of revival with deliverances and healings. Men and women who had larger churches than I'd ever set foot in prayed for the people who came forward. These leaders got behind a kid from Pennsylvania who did not even know he was a *profeta*! They saw something in me that I did not see. They saw who God had already said I was, and they gave me *permission to be that*.

Afterward, a group of pastors prayed for me. The lead pastor said, "Profeta, you come back. We're going to have a *cosecha* (harvest) in seventeen cities around our nation. We want you to be in one of those cities."

Six months later, in Venezuela, I saw posters announcing "Cosecha 2002." All the speakers' names were Hispanic, except for one: Bob Hazlett.

It looked hilarious in that sea of vowels, but it was wonderful, and I'll never forget it. In fact, I still have that framed poster!

The night before we were dispatched to our assigned cities, the apostle told me, "Profeta, I'm sending you to the most difficult city in Venezuela."

I said, "Thank you, apóstol," with some irony in my voice.

"I'm sending you because you're a profeta. That's what is needed to open up difficult places."

I replied, "OK. I guess so."

The apostle said, "You're going to Barquisimeto, the 'City of Revolutions.' Every major societal, political, or spiritual revolution in our country involves Barquisimeto. Venezuela's last revival was forty years ago this week, and it happened in that city. It ended there, too, because the churches didn't come together. Instead, they became divided."

Then he said something that was life-changing for me: "An evangelist from America named T. L. Osborn ministered in the revival in Barquisimeto. I'm sending you back to start it up again."

"What?" I pictured myself in the hallway of my childhood home, crying over the T. L. Osborn book.

Tears of intercession had indeed watered the seeds of destiny. Now permission had been released. It was connected to other people's permission, just as God's promises are connected to other people's promises. The apostle verbalized the connection. "Forty years ago, blind eyes opened and deaf ears heard," he said. "People walked out of their wheelchairs. God is going to do the same thing through you."

My head was spinning, but I believed the apostle. On the first night in Barquisimeto, I said, "There's somebody here who's deaf. You've been deaf since you were young, but you're going to hear tonight."

I heard a scream from the back and thought, *That was quick!*

The pastor's wife grabbed hold of a twenty-one-year-old woman from the dance team and practically dragged her forward. Then the pastor's wife said, "This young girl was saved seven years ago. The day she was saved, there was a prophecy in our church that, in seven years, there would be a citywide revival, and in that revival her ears would be opened—and it would be a sign that God was opening the ears of this nation!"

What could I say? God had said this would happen. I believed it, and God did it. My only part was to act on His authorization. Permission had been granted multiple times: to me at age fourteen; to the apostle, as a promise of revival; and to the young woman who had received a word seven years earlier. There was nothing to fear, and no reason to wait. There was only one way I could have messed up something God had spoken so many times—I could have refused to act at all.

Follow Someone to Your Promise

Dreams are rarely fulfilled in "tulip patches." Often, they blossom in "war zones." That was how it worked in the life of Daniel, a Hebrew in the Babylonian captivity who had been given a position as one of the king's "wise men." Daniel held on to a promise that most of the people in captivity had abandoned—the promise of the Israelites returning to their land, where the temple would be rebuilt and God's presence would dwell among His people again.

The situation in Babylon looked nothing like the promise. Yet Daniel watched for opportunities. One came when King Nebuchadnezzar had a troubling dream.

> *Then the astrologers answered the king, "May the king live forever! Tell your servants the dream, and we will interpret it." The king replied to the astrologers, "This is what I have firmly decided: If you do not tell me what my dream was and interpret it, I will have you cut into pieces and your houses turned into piles of rubble. But if you tell me the dream and explain it, you will receive from me gifts and rewards and great honor. So tell me the dream and interpret it for me."* (Daniel 2:4–6)

The astrologers argued the impossibility of the king's request—to no avail. In anger and frustration, Nebuchadnezzar ordered the deaths of all the wise men in the kingdom, including Daniel and his friends. Daniel's steps seemed hopelessly cluttered. Yet opportunity was knocking, and

Daniel saw it! The king's dream was troubling; all he really wanted was for someone to give meaning to it.

Daniel was the man for the job. After hearing about the king's execution orders, he stepped up.

> Daniel went in to the king and asked for time, so that he might interpret the dream for him. Then Daniel returned to his house and explained the matter to his friends Hananiah, Mishael and Azariah. He urged them to plead for mercy from the God of heaven concerning this mystery, so that he and his friends might not be executed with the rest of the wise men of Babylon. (Daniel 2:16–18)

God put Daniel in Nebuchadnezzar's life to tell him what his dream meant and to reveal the One who provided the answer. The king felt threatened by his dream; but Daniel's dream (the promise from God of Israel's restoration) was threatened by the king. So, God brought the two men together. Daniel would solve the riddle of the king's dream, and Nebuchadnezzar would use his position to facilitate Daniel's move to his next level.

Daniel understood the dynamics. He was thinking like heaven! He found a man who walked in favor and occupied high places, and he followed him—*by blessing him.*

Notice that Daniel did not judge the king or discredit his blessings. Nor did Daniel complain about his own situation. Daniel wanted to use his spiritual influence to help the king. It was God's idea, so God "showed up":

> During the night the mystery was revealed to Daniel in a vision. Then Daniel praised the God of heaven and said: "Praise be to the name of God for ever and ever; wisdom and power are his. He changes times and seasons; he deposes kings and raises up others. He gives wisdom to the wise and knowledge to the discerning. He reveals deep and hidden things; he knows what lies in darkness, and light dwells with him. I thank and praise you, God of my ancestors: You have given me wisdom and power, you have made known to me what we asked of you, you have made known to us the dream of the king." (Daniel 2:19–23)

Daniel essentially prayed, "Lord, I want to be where You have called me to be—in the place promised for my people. This isn't it, but I know this: You don't just set the times and seasons. You change them, and people, too!"

Daniel saw the shift coming. He trusted God to clear away the clutter and to bring the right people into his life. When a new level awaits you, God sends people who can take you there. He brings in His resources and changes circumstances to serve His purpose. His permission and His provision work together.

Far-out Dreaming

God's dreams are so far-out that they often trouble us at first. As we learn to trust Him, He meets us and guides us up the steps. If, instead, we remain fearful, our permission goes unused and our dreams go unfulfilled. Our failure to launch will affect many people, if only because we will nullify their dreams as surely as we have discounted our own.

God wants to clean our steps so we can help other people to clean theirs. He is training us to think like heaven so we can do the impossible and show others that they can do it, too. When we are "stuck," we need to connect with people who have moved past the place we are in. God will use them to escort us into higher places.

The Helper in Your Crisis

With my first book, I thought writing was the hard part. I found out that editing was harder. The closer the deadline came, the more mistakes I found. One day, I felt frazzled and asked my daughter April to look over the manuscript and to correct any mistakes.

April saw the frazzle in my eyes and said, "Dad, you need to go outside, talk a walk, and talk to God."

I thought, *Who's the parent here?*

April was right. I started walking and said, "God, I don't understand. I've worked so hard on this book, but it's not working. How are we going to do this?"

He said, "Why don't you ask Me which part of My nature I want to reveal in this situation? You're trying to get a book done, but I'm trying to show you something about Me."

It was what Daniel saw: "You're the God who changes times and seasons. You raise up kings and depose them. You give wisdom to the wise." In other words, "I have a problem, but the answer is more than an editing solution. It's discovering who You are in the middle of this problem."

Problems give us permission to learn something about God we never knew before. We are quick to ask Him to fix the problem, but He came to do something bigger than that.

We say, "Lord, I need money."

He says, "I am your Provider."

"I need healing, Lord."

"I am your Healer."

What I wanted was nothing compared to *who He is*. So, I surrendered and asked Him, "What do You want to reveal about Yourself?"

He said something simple but profound: "I like to help."

"*What?*"

"I'm a Helper. That's one of My names. I'm a very present help in your time of need." (See Psalm 46:1 NKJV, KJV.)

Because I am more visual than verbal, He showed me a picture. He and I were on a football field, but He was on the bench, watching, and I was the quarterback. I hiked the ball to myself and then handed it off to myself. Then I threw a flea-flicker, caught it, and tossed a lateral back to myself. Finally, I threw myself a Hail Mary and tackled myself!

He said, "That's what you're doing. You're playing every position, and I'm on the bench, saying, 'Put Me in the game.'"

"So, what should I do?" I asked.

"Ask Me to help."

"Is it really that simple?"

"Yes. Just ask Me."

I grew up believing that asking for help was a sign of weakness. So, I became a "do-it-myselfer." I was the clutter on my stairs. You can't get to the next level by yourself. Daniel knew that. He asked for his friends' support, and He looked to God and acknowledged aloud all that God would do. He called on the Helper and put himself in the Helper's hands.

Something supernatural happened when Daniel prayed the following:

I thank and praise you, God of my ancestors: You have given me wisdom and power, you have made known to me what we asked of you, you have made known to us the dream of the king. (Daniel 2:23)

What Daniel said about God (see Daniel 2:20) had become true of Daniel! That is why God shows us Himself—so we can see that we are like Him. Then we can stop defining ourselves by our limitations and start defining ourselves by our Father's strengths.

You are ready for the next level not because you are an experienced do-it-yourselfer but because God lives in you and is ready to take you there. He will often bring in a third party who is already at the level you are about to reach. Sow into that person's dreams, and your dream will come alive.

Thankful in Advance

Daniel wisely connected with Nebuchadnezzar in their mutual time of need. Years later, Babylon was ruled by a Persian named Darius, under whose reign a decree was issued commanding all subjects to worship him. Anyone who refused or who worshipped someone else would be thrown into the lions' den to be devoured.

Have you ever been in a situation that went from bad to worse? Did the recession hit your sector harder than most? Did others seem to recover while you continued to struggle? Have you held on to a promise, only to see it fulfilled in everybody's life but yours? Have your children gotten mixed up with the wrong crowd and gone haywire?

You can probably relate to the deteriorating situation Daniel faced. So, what did he do? *He gave thanks.* His dream seemed no closer, and the threat of death stalked him once again. He stood at the bottom of his steps, looking up, and found a way to see past the clutter. Heaven's thinking was in Daniel's heart.

> *Now when Daniel learned that the decree had been published, he went home to his upstairs room where the windows opened toward Jerusalem. Three times a day he got down on his knees and prayed, giving thanks to his God, just as he had done before.* (Daniel 6:10)

He went to where his windows opened toward Jerusalem, because Jerusalem was where his promise was. He faced his dream, but all he saw in front of him was Babylonian desert dirt. So, three times a day, he hit his knees and gave thanks—"*just as he had done before*"!

Nothing changed. The decree remained in effect. But God also remained on His throne. A law could not nullify His promise. Daniel's job was to maintain an "upstairs perspective." Instead of looking down his nose and criticizing the people and the things in his way, Daniel gave thanks for the truth that superseded all circumstances.

Thanksgiving opens up atmospheres. Worship opens a window to your promise. Daniel did not withhold his thanksgiving until the promise came. He worshipped and gave thanks in advance. That is thinking like heaven.

Suffering, Perseverance, Character, and Hope

To the world, the definition of insanity is doing the same thing over and over and expecting different results. Yet, in regard to spiritual realities, God says that is the definition of faith! We are to keep doing what God said to do. It's called *persistence*.

Paul explained this idea in Romans:

Therefore, since we have been justified through faith, we have peace with God through our Lord Jesus Christ, through whom we have gained access by faith into this grace in which we now stand. And we boast in the hope of the glory of God. Not only so, but we also glory in our sufferings, because we know that suffering produces perseverance; perseverance, character; and character, hope. And hope does not put us to shame, because God's love has been poured out into our hearts through the Holy Spirit, who has been given to us. (Romans 5:1–5)

The word *"sufferings"* doesn't sound very encouraging, yet the passage is full of hope. Paul said that faith brings us into grace, and grace sustains us. So, what faith activates, grace empowers. Then hope explodes in our hearts so that we may *"glory in our sufferings."*

Really?

Really. Suffering trains us to persevere, which causes us to grow in character. The yield of character is hope, which does not disappoint. That means it doesn't cancel an appointment. Hope doesn't take God's promises off your calendar. Hope *nails* His promises to your calendar!

The reign of King David is a perfect example. His stairs were crammed with obstacles. His own father essentially blocked his path to the throne. And when David was about to stand up to Goliath, his oldest brother trash-talked him:

When Eliab…heard [David] speaking with the men, he burned with anger at him and asked, "Why have you come down here? And with whom did you leave those few sheep in the wilderness? I know how conceited you are and how wicked your heart is; you came down only to watch the battle." "Now what have I done?" said David. "Can't I even speak?"   (1 Samuel 17:28–29)

After David's victory over Goliath, King Saul became envious of him and hunted him down *for years.* David's stairway to the throne seemed impassable and was full of suffering, but he persevered. He became strong in character, and hope filled his heart. His hope did not disappoint. Every obstacle was leveled, and God's promise was fulfilled.

David thought like heaven!

The world system says suffering produces despair; but, in the kingdom, suffering—what happens when your reality and God's promise don't match—produces hope. You still believe the promise, but you ache for its manifestation. It seems all wrong, but suffering is integral to the supernatural. I'm not talking about God making you sick to teach you something or to inspire a good sermon. I'm talking about believing to the point that perseverance becomes your new default. Instead of complaining, quitting, or biting off people's heads, you smile and thank God for the opportunity to grow.

Until God healed her, my wife suffered from a physical ailment. Her healing convinced me that God would heal other people. At the time, I was on the staff of a church where prayer for the sick was not done. About two hours from my church, I found a church whose pastor believed in healing, and I asked whether he would agree to hold healing meetings. He said he would, so we decided to have meetings one Friday each month.

"What should we call the meetings?" he asked.

I said, "I don't know."

He said, "How about 'Friday Night Fire'!"

That sounded good to me. I thought, *People will come if fire is involved.*

Twenty people showed up for the first meeting. It didn't take long to line them up. Then I prayed for each one, and nobody got healed. I suffered because I knew there were more than twenty sick people in the area, and I knew God healed the sick. The truth did not match the reality we experienced.

With trepidation, I asked the pastor, "Do you want to do it again next month?"

"Sure," he said.

A new group of twenty people showed up. They lined up, and I prayed for them. Nobody got healed. The third and fourth months were the same way. Friday Night Fire felt more like "Friday Night Suffering"! Yet we kept doing what we had started out to do. At our fifth meeting, we repeated the drill. People lined up for prayer, and nobody was getting healed.

By the time I approached the last person in line, my expectations were very low. I asked the man, "What's going on?"

He explained that he'd just had three discs fused. "I'm wearing a back brace. I got out of the hospital yesterday."

I looked at the pastor. His body language said, *Don't look at me.*

I asked the man, "Is it OK if I pray for you?"

He said, "Yes."

As I prayed, I laid my hands on him and commanded every disc to be healed and all pain to go. Then I asked, "Sir, do you feel anything?"

"Yeah, it feels better," he said.

"Really?"

"Yeah, I think so."

He started moving around to test his back. I tried to slow him down, afraid that he might hurt himself, but he kept moving. Then he removed his brace, which made me nervous. He insisted, so I asked him to do something he could not do before we prayed.

He bent over. I needed more convincing, so I asked him to do something else. He insisted that he was healed. It seemed that he was more convinced than I was! It wasn't that I lacked faith. Faith is what had caused me to endure the monthly meetings and to continue in prayer. Persistence in prayer had then yielded perseverance—a relentless tenacity that formed new character within me. My new default in the face of apparent defeat was to *keep praying*! Then character did what it always does: It blossomed into fruit—not just healing for the man's back, but a new expectation that when I prayed, God would heal. In other words, I had hope! I also learned that hope sometimes comes only after God blows away my expectations.

Thinking like heaven changes us. It helps us to see the pain, problems, and injustice we suffer in a new light. Under the Roman culture, Christians endured much suffering, but Paul taught them a new perspective. Here's how *The Message* Bible puts it:

> By entering through faith into what God has always wanted to do for us—set us right with him, make us fit for him—we have it all together with God because of our Master Jesus. And that's not all: We throw open our doors to God and discover at the same moment that he has already thrown open his door to us. We find ourselves standing where we always hoped we might stand—out in the wide open spaces of God's grace and glory, standing tall and shouting our praise. There's more to come: We continue to shout our praise even when we're hemmed in with troubles, because we know how troubles can develop passionate patience in us, and how that patience in turn forges the tempered steel of virtue, keeping us alert for whatever God will do next. In alert expectancy such as this, we're never left feeling shortchanged. Quite the contrary—we can't round up enough containers to hold everything God generously pours into our lives through the Holy Spirit! Christ arrives right on time to make this happen. **He didn't, and doesn't, wait for us to get ready. He presented himself for this sacrificial death when we were far too weak and rebellious to do anything to get ourselves ready.** And even if we hadn't been so weak, we wouldn't have known what to do anyway. We can understand someone dying for a person worth dying for, and we can understand how someone good and noble could inspire us to selfless sacrifice. But God put his love on the line for us by offering his Son in sacrificial death while we were of no use whatever to him.   (Romans 5:1–8 MSG)

Do you feel as if you are stranded in Babylon, overwhelmed by clutter, and fresh out of hope? Guess what? Your appointment has not been canceled! God is preparing your steps and waiting for you to hear Him. He is handing you the keys and saying, "I have given you permission to be what you already are. You are more ready than you think. Come on. Let's go upstairs."

Thinking like Heaven

1. What did "permission" mean to you before reading this chapter? How has your understanding of this concept expanded? Ask God to show you the permission He has given you to become who and what you already are in Christ.

2. Have you cried tears of intercession? Had you forgotten about them till now? God wants to bring them to your mind. Just ask Him. He remembers every tear. He sowed each one into your future.

3. Ask God to reveal an area in which you are afraid—whether consciously or unconsciously—to move forward because you think you will mess up. Let Him show you the times and the ways in which He has confirmed His permission for you to proceed. Then consider what *not* acting will mean.

4. Is God connecting you with a "Nebuchadnezzar"? Ask Him what He has in mind and what your mutual roles are.

5. Are you a "do-it-yourselfer"? Ask God to reveal the root of your behavior, and He will show you how to change. Then thank Him in advance for teaching you to ask for His help.

9

Fearless

Basketball is one of my favorite games, and the University of Connecticut is my team. In 2014, the Huskies beat the Wildcats, their archrival from the University of Kentucky. It was a huge win. The day after the victory, I left for a conference in Lexington, Kentucky, of all places, and I wore my UConn cap, as I often do. When I stepped off the plane and into the terminal, people stared at me. *Yeah,* I thought, *I've lost a little weight. I must be looking good.* I was momentarily oblivious to the stir my hat was causing.

When I called the organizer of the conference to tell him I had arrived, he said, "All right. Let's get something to eat."

He had my favorite food in mind—Buffalo Wild Wings.

I thought, *Hallelujah and pass the Mango Habanero.*

The restaurant happened to serve the University of Kentucky campus. For someone wearing UConn colors, that was enemy territory. I was glad to be traveling with a friend who is well over six feet tall. My confidence waned when we arrived at the eatery and found fifteen or twenty guys milling around the entrance. They had obviously consumed mass quantities of wings and liquid spirits and were trying to tip over a car.

The leader said, "Yo. Help us tip this car."

He probably thought my very tall friend would be a car-tipping machine. Then he noticed my hat. "You—UConn," he said.

The guy seemed menacing. My friend pulled an Enoch: One second he was with me; the next, he disappeared into thin air.

"UConn!" the leader repeated.

It was game on, and I was outmatched. My mind was running through fight-or-flight scenarios when a third response presented itself: a word of knowledge.

For the third time, the leader shouted, "UConn!"

This time, I answered him. "Your shoulder," I said.

He said, "What the ____!" (It didn't sound like "hallelujah.")

I said, "You hurt your shoulder in a construction accident three years ago."

He said, "Holy ____," as the other guys gave animated "signs and wonders" and spoke in funky, unknown "tongues."

"How did you know that?" he asked.

I answered, "I am going to pray for you."

Laying hands on the sick is a good thing to do, but I opted to speak to this particular "mountain." I knew that if he didn't get healed, I would need a head start running. "I command your shoulder to be healed in Jesus' name."

He felt something, and it freaked him out. "How did you do that?"

"I'm just a believer in Jesus," I said. "He likes to listen to our prayers."

Magically, my friend reappeared, and we walked into the restaurant. The leader of the pack followed us inside. Thinking I was a priest, he asked, "Father, how did you do that?"

I told him that God had created him and loved him and wanted to change his life. He opened up about his job and other things. Then he gave his life to Christ—right there in Buffalo Wild Wings!

What Fearlessness Looks Like

Being fearless doesn't mean ignoring danger. It means thinking like heaven so that fight and flight aren't your only options. If fear had commandeered my thinking, the encounter with the car-tipping gang could have gone south in a hurry. Instead, I was able to hold fast in "enemy territory" and turn my opponents into friends. My fearlessness wasn't about personal bravery. It was based in righteousness—*Christ's* righteousness *in me*. I did not have to appease anyone, deny who I was, or change my clothes. I was free to stand firm and to listen for heaven's instructions.

Fearlessness is power. With fear broken off your life, you can run boldly toward your destiny, regardless of the obstacles. You see what God sees, and, because you are bold, you become it.

That is what Peter did on the Sea of Galilee. When he realized that the "ghost" walking past the disciples' boat was Jesus, he said, *"Lord, if it is You, command me to come to You on the water"* (Matthew 14:28 NASB). That was bold! Peter saw Jesus doing the impossible and figured he could do it, too. His courage did not come from self-confidence; it came from what he saw Jesus doing. It's not as though Peter wasn't human. There was probably a moment when he thought walking on the water might cost him his life. But he was thinking like heaven. He saw God's bigger picture, and he entered it.

Fulfilling our destiny demands that we take steps into the unknown. God draws us into situations that look impossible in order to stretch our faith and to make us tenacious. He's not looking for an army of thrill-seeking daredevils. He simply wants us to see what He sees, so that we will do what we thought was impossible and fulfill His kingdom purposes.

Fearlessness releases the miraculous. Notice what happened after the walking-on-water encounter: "[The disciples] *willingly received* [Jesus] *into the boat, and **immediately** the boat was at the land where they were going"* (John 6:21 NKJV). The balance of their journey was accelerated, and they reached their destination instantaneously! After their rough night at sea, I'm sure the disciples were thrilled with this result. But I believe their miraculous arrival happened because Peter saw what God wanted to do. His boldness reaped more of a miracle than any of them expected.

Being fearless means knowing *whose* you are. Do you remember those rats we talked about that grew receptors that enabled them to be brave? "Foster mothers" nurtured them, and they became bold.[1] That's what happens when you dwell *"in the secret place of the Most High"*—you *"abide under the shadow of the Almighty"* and are not afraid *"of the pestilence that walks in darkness, nor of the destruction that lays waste at noonday"* (Psalm 91:1, 6 NKJV). You become fearless under your heavenly Father's nurturing. Even if you were raised in a fearful home environment, you were born again into a fearless one—and you have all the courage receptors you will ever need.

Fearless by Identity

Scripture gives numerous examples of overly fearful people and brilliantly fearless ones. Proverbs 28:1 juxtaposes both: *"The wicked flee though no one pursues, but the righteous are as bold as a lion."* *Wicked* doesn't refer only to wrong actions; it means being twisted or perverted in one's identity. In this case, the wicked see themselves as being powerless. They don't realize who they are. They are blind to their divine resources. So, they flee for no reason at all.

Recently, I heard a preacher say something that struck me. He said that we have been taught to confess our sins over and over until we "feel better"; but, instead of confessing our sins, we ought to confess our righteousness. I believe both confessions are healthy. If you mess up, "fess up" and then keep believing what God says about you. On the cross, Jesus became sin, and He made you righteous. Spend more time thinking about who you *are* instead of who you *are not*. No wonder the wicked flee when no one is chasing them. They are tangled up in who they are not!

When we are driven by wicked (earthly) mind-sets, we run from the situations God wants us to confront. He allows us to be stretched so that we can learn to face difficult situations and transform them. With a

Fearless 167

righteous perspective of heaven and of ourselves, we can run boldly at our challenges and recognize God's purposes in them.

In Numbers 13, when ten of the twelve Israelite spies whined about the dangers of the Promised Land, including the giants who lived there, Caleb said, *"We should go up and take possession of the land, for we can certainly do it"* (Numbers 13:30). Caleb (as well as Joshua) was ready to take on the opposition. He said, in effect, "Don't be afraid of them. *They are bread for us*'!" (See Numbers 14:9 KJV). The fearful spies saw themselves as prey, but Caleb saw himself as predator. He was as bold as a lion!

That kind of fearlessness does not come from your personality or your circumstances. It comes from your identity. Caleb knew who he was—a man sent by the Most High to take the territory. He did not need a business card or an ordination certificate to feel important or empowered. He did not need the affirmation and approval of others to become and to do all that God had destined him to become and to do.

You don't need these things, either. You are *"God's handiwork, created in Christ Jesus to do good works, which God prepared in advance for* [you] *to do"* (Ephesians 2:10). With *"Christ in you, the hope of glory"* (Colossians 1:27), being fearless comes "naturally."

Fearlessness in Action

Though he faced a nine-foot-tall giant in heavy armor, David was fearless. Nurtured in God's presence, he had learned to face down wild animals. Now, he was prepared to take down the warrior who made Israel's entire army—and even its king—tremble. Wearing no armor, and with no weapons but a slingshot and some stones, David ran straight toward Goliath and took him out.

Centuries later, Jesus faced the cross with the same tenacity. It was a deadly assignment, but He took it head-on. He went into enemy territory, gave His life for His enemies, and made them His friends—multiplied millions of them!

Fearlessness Looks Forward

Fearless people are willing to look into unseen realms, believing they can bring what God has revealed into plain sight. They are forward-looking and focused not on the past but on the horizon.

Fixation on the past is anathema to the future. When Samuel went to Jesse's house to anoint the next king of Israel, the prophet was influenced by past experiences and perceptions. Seeing David's oldest brother, Eliab, he thought, *"Surely the* Lord's *anointed stands here before the* Lord*"* (1 Samuel 16:6).

King Saul was tall, and so was Eliab. He looked "right" for the job, but he was not God's man for the throne. Samuel's near misread is interesting, because Scripture says, *"The* Lord *was with Samuel as he grew up, and he let none of Samuel's words fall to the ground"* (1 Samuel 3:19). How did a prophet as accurate as Samuel get sidetracked by appearances? Simple: He was momentarily focused on what the past had taught him. The once-anointed King Saul was "tall, dark, and handsome." (See 1 Samuel 9:2.) Now, Samuel mourned the failure of Saul's kingship and almost reproduced that failure by choosing someone because he looked the same as Saul. While David's qualities might not have appeared to be kingly at first glance, God thought they were great!

Thankfully, God got the prophet's attention:

The Lord *said to Samuel, "Do not consider [Eliab's] appearance or his height, for I have rejected him. The* Lord *does not look at the things people look at. People look at the outward appearance, but the* Lord *looks at the heart."*   (1 Samuel 16:7)

God saw in David the qualities He desired in His future king. David's fear response had been transformed by God into boldness. The day was coming when his big brother Eliab would cower in fear of Goliath while David shouted, *"Who is this uncircumcised Philistine that he should defy the armies of the living God?"* (1 Samuel 17:26).

David's boldness did not come overnight. It was developed through persistence. When David told Saul about the lion and the bear that he had killed, he didn't mention how many lions had clawed his backside before that! David had no doubt encountered numerous predators, and some encounters had probably turned out better than others. But, at some point, David got over his past and became bold enough to say, "I tried that, and it failed, but I'm getting back up to try again. I was hated by those who should have loved me, but I'm headed for victory anyway." Like the righteous who fall seven times, David rose again. (See Proverbs 24:16.)

Boldness from Heaven to Earth

One Sunday morning, I was preaching in Australia, and a woman with a thick scar on her left wrist came to the front with her parents. Her hand was frozen in place, so I asked her what had happened. She said, "When I was four years old, I had an accident that cut the tendons in my wrist. This is the way it healed."

I said, "The Bible says the prayer of faith will save the sick, so let's pray."

I put my hand on her wrist and said, "In the name of Jesus, I speak to these tendons to be healed. I command this hand to be opened, in Jesus' name." Then I asked the woman to open her hand.

She tried and said, "I can't."

I was disappointed, but boldness prays again, so I did. I had to see the situation from God's perspective, with His end result in mind. If I took any other view, I would be tempted to protect my reputation and make excuses for why the first prayer hadn't worked. I might even have told the young woman that she needed more faith, when all I needed was to believe that the sick will recover when I lay my hands on them. (See Mark 16:18.)

So, I put my hand on her wrist again. This time, I saw a picture of her playing the piano with both hands, writing a song, and singing. When I told her what I saw, she began to cry and said, "I just started taking piano lessons a year ago." Her mother nodded, and the young woman continued, "I am only able to play with one hand."

It was clear what God wanted to do, so I prayed, "God, I thank You for two brand-new piano hands. I thank You for a gift to sing and write." Then I told her, "Now try it out."

Her hand opened up. She was healed!

Faith, Hope, Love, and Boldness

Second Corinthians 3:12 says, *"Therefore, since we have such a hope, we are very bold."* Sometimes, we think we are bold because we step out in faith. But boldness comes from hope, which allows us to see what God wants to do. Then we attach our faith to whatever God reveals, and it becomes *"the substance of things hoped for"* (Hebrews 11:1 NKJV, KJV). The unseen becomes visible when we become bold.

In the same meeting, a boy who was perhaps eleven years old came forward with his parents. Next to him was a lady with a walker (or a cane, I can't remember which). So, I said to his family, "Can I pray for this woman first, and then pray for you guys?"

They said, "Absolutely."

I asked the older woman, "What do you need, ma'am?"

She said, "I'm supposed to have two knee-replacement surgeries soon. I need my two knees replaced by God."

I looked at the boy and asked, "Have you ever seen someone healed before?"

He said, "Never."

I said, "Watch this."

As I turned to pray, the Lord stopped me. "No," He said. "Have the boy pray for her."

"Have you ever prayed for someone to be healed?" I asked the boy.

"Nope. Never."

I said, "Come on, let's do it."

We got on our knees together, and I walked him through the prayer. He said, "In Jesus' name, I command this knee to be healed."

The woman lifted up her right knee and said, "That's much, much better."

Before I could suggest praying for the left knee, the boy commanded her left knee to be healed.

I worked myself out of a job that day! After I left Australia, but before I landed back in the States, I received two messages. One was from the girl whose frozen hand had been healed. She said, "I went home today and played the piano with two hands for the first time. And I wrote my first song today."

The second message was from the mother of the young boy. She said, "Thank you for praying for us. What you said really encouraged us. But you changed my son's life by letting him pray for that woman. On the way home from the meeting, he wanted to stop and pray for the sick."

God asked me a question: "Which of those miracles do you think is better?"

"I don't know," I answered. "They're both pretty awesome. I don't want to rank them, but the creative miracle is amazing. And I really liked the one with the little boy because he got involved in ministering, too."

God asked, "Why is that so great?"

"Well, because he's going to think it's normal to pray for the sick."

"No, it is even better than that," He said. "The first time he saw someone healed, it was because someone taught him how to heal and pray for the sick. He thinks it is normal to teach people how to do those things."

That's how we raise a fearless generation!

At a series of meetings in Florence, Alabama, five churches came together. On the final night, during praise and worship, the Lord gave me ten words of knowledge for specific healings. I thought I would preach the message, then bring forth these words and pray for the sick. When the time came, the Lord said, "I don't want you to pray for the sick. I want you to have the children pray for the sick."

When I asked all the children age ten and younger to come forward, more than thirty stepped up. I told them, "God is going to give you some words of knowledge. Then we are going to call them out." I briefly explained further and then prayed a quick prayer.

Immediately, ten fearless kids raised their hands and started calling out words of knowledge. By the time the third child spoke, I realized that everything they were calling out was on the list God had given me during praise and worship!

I remember thinking about a certain item that no one had touched on yet. It involved a girl who was having trouble breathing because of a cracked rib. No sooner had the thought come to mind than the very next child—a girl maybe nine years old—pointed to her rib cage and said, "I feel a pain right here. When I breathe, it really hurts."

It was *amazing*. She had perceived another person's need. The girl whose rib really was cracked responded to the nine-year-old girl's word of knowledge and was healed!

Next, an eight-year-old girl unknowingly addressed another word on my list. It was for a man with three bad disks in his back. When the man came forward, I told the girl to thank Jesus for giving the man a new back. She did, and the man was healed!

The Young and the Righteous

If we teach our kids at a young age who they are, the world will not succeed in telling them otherwise. They won't identify themselves by church labels, denominations, or educational or economic backgrounds. They will simply say, "I am Jesus' kid, and I believe I can heal. I can lay hands on the sick, and they will recover." Best of all, they will never, ever question who God is. They will only believe Him.

Welcome, Fearless One!

When you know who you are, and when you see what God sees, you make no excuses for being fearless. Your boldness comes from His righteousness in you. You don't need a "courage pill" or psychotherapy. You don't even need a supportive earthly family. All you need is the love and support of the One who created you. You are His child, and He is grooming you under the shelter of His wing.

Many psychologists say that firstborn children are more assertive than their siblings because they get the most nurturing. In God's kingdom, every child is a "firstborn child," with equal access to the Father's nurturing love. All of us can be bold because we were all in Christ from the foundation of the world. In Him, none of us went unnurtured or unloved, and none of us was wounded or broken.

Each of us has been called to do something. It might seem as impossible as walking on water—but, with Him, it can be done.

God says, "Come. I will enable you to do and to be *everything* I have called you to do and to be. In Me, you are *fearless.*"

Thinking like Heaven

1. Under what circumstances are you most likely to be bold? Ask God to reveal the source of your boldness. What surprises you about His response?

2. Are there areas of life or certain settings in which you feel powerless? In your opinion, what is the root of this feeling? Ask God to reveal how He has empowered you. How does His answer refute your feelings?

3. Think of a time when you evaluated a person or a situation on the basis of old mind-sets. Compare/contrast your example with the prophet Samuel's first impression of Eliab.

4. How would you feel if you prayed for someone to be healed, and nothing happened? What would your response be? What informs this response?

5. Which seems more intimidating to you: praying for the sick or teaching others to pray for the sick? What does your sense of intimidation put at risk?

Notes

1. See, for example, Regina Sullivan, Ph.D., and Elizabeth Norton Lasley, "Fear in Love: Attachment, Abuse, and the Developing Brain," *Cerebrum*, September 1, 2010, U.S. National Library of Medicine, National Institutes of Health, http://www.ncbi.nlm.nih.gov/pmc/articles/PMC3574772/, and Stephanie Moriceau and Regina M. Sullivan, "Maternal Presence Serves as a Switch Between Learning Fear and Attraction in Infancy," NIH Public Access Author Manuscript, U.S. National Library of Medicine, National Institutes of Health, July 9, 2006, http://www.ncbi.nlm.nih.gov/pmc/articles/PMC1560090/.

10

Living from Surplus

Bob Hazlett @bob_hazlett
Do something BIG today: Tip a little extra, listen a little more, take a small step toward a large dream. #ThinklikeHeaven #LivefromSurplus

↩ ⇄ ★ •••

know I cannot *really live* without God. I can only exist and plod along. Even having what I call the "best job in the world," I need Him desperately. Traveling the globe in His name is *phenomenal*, but the logistics alone are miles above my pay grade. Without Him, I would not know where or how to begin, and I would have little to offer.

Not long ago, I was in Berlin, and I left my hotel room at 4:00 AM to catch a flight to Washington, D.C. Twenty hours later, I landed in D.C., and one hour after that, I was scheduled to be in another meeting. My itinerary was so tight, it squeaked.

Fatigued and with luggage in tow, I met the taxi driver who would take me to my hotel. He popped his trunk and looked at me. Then his eyes moved away from mine and toward my luggage. Next, they darted toward his trunk and back to me, as though signaling what he wanted me to do. The new creation part of me stayed mellow, but the "old man" within me considered how this game might lower his tip. I caught myself and told the old, dead part to shut up. Then I put my luggage in the trunk.

From the backseat of the cab, I saw the driver's name and country of origin. I guessed that his religion disapproved of my faith. My natural mind surmised his opinion of me and assumed that it explained his attitude. While I considered his fleshly behavior, my assessments were guided by *my* flesh. If I had acted on them, I would have treated him with equal disregard.

Instead, I dipped into heaven's resources and decided that I would bless him, no matter what. It was only a three- or four-minute drive to the hotel, but I planned to give him a nice, fat tip. I flipped past the smaller bills in my wallet and pulled out a bigger one. When we arrived at our destination, he popped the trunk and repeated his silent treatment, moving his eyes in the same strange ways as before.

That's when the Holy Spirit intervened. He said, "He can't pick up your bag because he hurt his arm."

I wasn't even trying to hear from God; He just poured it out, as though saying, "Dude, you really need some help here. Just ask the man if he's injured."

"Sir," I said, "did you hurt yourself?"

"Yes. Three weeks ago, I fell and sprained the tendons in my arm. That's why I can't pick up your bag."

He showed me the brace on his arm. I said, "Can I see that for a second?" Normally, I ask for permission to pray. In this case, I just asked to see his hand, took hold of it, and prayed, "In Jesus' name, I command this arm to be healed and these tendons to be loosed." Then I let go and said, "Sir, how does it feel?"

"Wow," he said. "That is much better!"

As he removed the brace and picked up my suitcase, I said, "The God of Abraham loves you." I figured we could agree on Abraham.

He liked that. "Thank you," he said. "The God of Abraham loves you, too."

Two people who have almost nothing in common can bless each other when at least one of them has insight from heaven.

Atmosphere Transformation

We live in this world, but we do not live from it. (See John 17:11, 14–18.) If we have been raised with Christ (see Colossians 3:1), we are invited to live from heaven. Earthly atmospheres might surround us, but we can soak in heaven's atmosphere and draw it into the earth.

This is not about pearly gates and chubby, naked-bottomed cherubs with harps. We have already seen the atmosphere of heaven described. It was when Isaiah saw *"the Lord, high and exalted, seated on a throne; and the train of his robe filled the temple"* (Isaiah 6:1). In an atmosphere of holiness and incessant praise, Isaiah's perspective was undone and his needs were met. He realized he was ruined by sin and desperate for God. The Lord then responded by cleansing him and filling him with heaven to fulfill His purposes in the earth. (See Isaiah 6:5–8.)

What a moment! God allowed Isaiah to see behind the veil, and it set his heart ablaze. That fire was the atmosphere of heaven, which Isaiah then brought to earth. Whether he was embraced or rejected by the people and the authorities he spoke to, Isaiah seeded heavenly atmospheres wherever he went.

That is what living from surplus does. It does not focus on lawmaking or on policing people's conduct. It simply spreads the holy contagion of heaven's thinking and allows justice to flow from it. That is what I believe God is doing. He is releasing His grace so that we can exhale the mind of Christ wherever we go. Atmospheres *will* shift as entire populations begin thinking like heaven.

Jesus is our example. He carried heaven's atmosphere to earth and changed world history. He did not remove Himself from the culture; He challenged groupthink by demonstrating the kingdom. For too long, the church has isolated itself from the world. We pulled out of politics and the educational system. We withdrew to "Christian quarters" where we felt comfortable and accepted, not realizing that we had abdicated our place of influence and withheld the atmosphere of heaven from those who desperately needed it.

We will never change the world by segregating ourselves from the culture. Certainly, Christian education and homeschooling serve important purposes, especially where children's safety is at risk. One of my daughters was homeschooled, and one attends public school. I'm not advocating either one or making a law out of it. The point is that Christian schools cannot transform secular education. The kingdom mind-set will not touch the secular system unless we take it there.

Notice how Isaiah 55:7 frames the issue of mind-sets:

Let the wicked forsake their ways and the unrighteous their thoughts.
Let them turn to the Lord, *and he will have mercy on them, and to our*
God, for he will freely pardon.

People's wicked ways are linked to their unrighteous thoughts. It is impossible to think like hell and act like heaven. The opposite is also true. If we can help the unrighteous to change their thinking, they will turn away from sin. When God said, *"My thoughts are not your thoughts, neither are your ways my ways"* (Isaiah 55:8), He didn't condemn the world to its darkness. Instead, He promised that His Word would water the earth with heaven's nourishment. (See Isaiah 55:10–11.)

And we are God's waterspouts! We don't need to whack people over the head with what He has given us. We need only pour out the atmosphere of heaven in their midst. Then His love will transform and refresh us all.

Contagious Thinking

As I write this, the Ebola virus has the world on edge. It is a wicked disease that can kill in a matter of days. It is highly contagious and has crossed national borders, particularly in western Africa.

Not all contagions result in swift, physical death. Thoughts can be "viral," too, spreading ideas that release subtle forms of death over time. In Matthew 9:4, Jesus addressed the malignant thinking of some religious leaders, saying, *"Why do you entertain evil thoughts in your hearts?"* The Greek word translated *"evil"* in this verse is *poneros*, which means "diseased."[1] The leaders' thinking had grown corrupt, and it was becoming contagious. The good news is that heavenly thinking has the antibodies for "stinking thinking."

Remember that we are carriers of the thoughts we entertain. Choose wisely, and heaven's thoughts will "infect" the earth.

Flowing from Heaven to Earth

Standing in line to board a flight one day, I had a conversation with God in my head—not realizing that I was actually speaking audibly. One guy gave me that "Who *are* you talking to?" kind of look. I was tempted to pull a Bluetooth fake and say, "Yeah…yeah…OK…I'll call you later" to a nonexistent person on the other end of the phone.

Apparently, the God-conversations in my head often go this way. The reality is that you do not have to disconnect from your heavenly conversation to have an earthly one. Even if you are poor at multitasking, you are wired to talk to God and to others at the same time.

I found this to be true while speaking at a large youth event in Germany. After asking a young girl to stand up, I said to her, "I see you as a very creative person who loves fashion and vintage clothing. I see you shopping for old clothing and turning it into something new. Then you take these old clothes and put them on poor people who are in need of clothing. I see God sending you to a foreign nation on a short trip next year so you can learn to love the poor and bring clothing to the needy."

It was a very encouraging word to her. I could tell because she was smiling and crying at the same time, and her friends were all cheering and clapping for her.

The next day, a group of young people approached me. They said that the young girl was their friend and that everything I had spoken about her was true. They asked me how I knew all that stuff about her. I simply answered, "God told me."

They wanted more specifics. One young man asked, "How does He talk to you?"

I explained it this way: "While I was talking to your friend, I was also talking to God, asking Him questions. It went like this…

"Q: 'God, how do You see her?'

"A: 'She is creative.'

"Q: 'How is she creative?'

"A: 'She likes fashion.'

"Q: 'What kind of fashion?'

"A: 'Vintage clothing.'

"Q: 'What will she do with it?'

"A: 'Clothe needy people.'

"Q: 'Where?'

"A: 'In a foreign country.'

"Q: 'When?'

"A: 'Next year.'"

Later, I heard that she did end up going on that mission trip, no doubt with an extra suitcase full of vintage clothing.

These in-my-head conversations demonstrate the continual flow of thoughts coming toward us. Not every thought comes from heaven. The enemy's accusing thoughts come and are disguised, so we assume they are *our* thoughts. Thoughts from adverse experiences tempt us to believe the worst about life and the future. Thoughts float in from the atmosphere and tend to reflect the climate of the place they came from. It is important to correctly identify these sources and then to focus on thoughts that come from heaven.

All of heaven's thoughts are good, but they are not "one size fits all." God is too creative for that! I recently went from a conference in Redding, California, to meetings in Oregon. Each place had a different cultural and spiritual climate and a unique destiny, so God spoke specifically to each place. During worship in Oregon, a friend of mine had a vision of a large saw—big enough to cut down redwood trees. He told me about it and asked, "What could that mean?"

I said, "I don't know about cutting down redwoods in the Northwest, but I think this used to be a logging area. Maybe God is releasing an industry that will be bigger than logging was."

Now I was curious, so I asked the pastor about the area. He said, "Yeah, logging was our biggest industry, but it's dead now."

I sensed that the congregation needed to hear about my friend's vision, so I asked him to share it. Then I told them what I believed it meant. "I believe that God is going to release something in this area, technologically and industry-wise, that's going to be bigger than the logging industry was."

There seemed to be more to it, so I asked the Lord to clarify. A picture opened up—a really weird picture of a hydroponic garden floating atop a boat. I began to prophesy, "Something is coming to this area...a technology from the Northwest and from San Francisco. It's as if Silicon Valley and Washington technology are meeting in this area, and the whole corridor will be involved. I saw industries coming—social awareness industries. I saw a hydroponic farm that could be transported to places where natural and man-made disasters have occurred. The farm will feed the hungry and provide clean food, even in a nuclear disaster."

Even as I prophesied, the words sounded crazy to me. After the service, three students from the Oregon Institute of Technology told the pastor, "We started a business just this week, and it's hydroponic farming. Our goal is to get it onto aircraft carriers that will serve natural disaster areas."

How awesome is that? A thought flowed from heaven that confirmed something I did not know God was already doing!

Don't be too quick to reject those "crazy" ideas that come to mind. It is so easy to think, *It's nothing. It's just me*, because it *is* you; but it is God speaking *through you*. You could be one crazy thought away from a world-changing idea, book, screenplay, song, business plan, or educational innovation that will transform a sector, a nation...the world.

God's Supply Is Endless

Getting out of our minds and into God's mind is a journey, and we are on it. The world's problems look different when we think like heaven. These problems started with worldly thinking, so how can they be solved by it? Worldly thoughts are based in limitation, lack, competition, and envy. The world sees all benefit in zero-sum terms that say, "If you have abundance, then I will have less." Heaven is not like that. Quantity and limitation are not heavenly concepts. God's supply is endless, and there is more than enough to meet every need, everywhere, every day.

One of my favorite Scriptures is Isaiah 55:1, which says, *"Come, buy wine and milk without money and without cost."* In my opinion, the idea of free stuff is heavenly. I suspect my view is partly genetic. I'm told that being of Pennsylvania Dutch heritage predisposes me to frugality. There is a favorite joke in the community: "Do you know how copper wire was invented? Two Pennsylvania Dutchmen got hold of a penny, and neither was willing to let go."

That's me. I can stretch a penny from sea to shining sea. Heaven doesn't work at stretching pennies. I'm not advocating wastefulness or stupidity with money. Heaven endorses neither. But in heaven, the standard is *surplus*, and the thinking follows suit.

We get preoccupied with our deficits, and we spend excessive amounts of energy trying to manage them. When God looks at us, He doesn't see deficits. He sees only Christ in us—and in Him, there is no shortage. But God is patient and understands the errors of our ways. So, He places us in atmospheres of greater deficits than the ones we are trying to master. Then He shows us His surplus—not "just enough" to meet our personal needs but enough to overflow and obliterate every deficit on all sides!

I live in Connecticut, a state that was rocked by two school tragedies in a relatively short span of time. The deficit in our culture is plain and painful. The mass murder in Newtown stunned the state and the nation.

Then our local community was shaken by another brutal crime as students prepared for prom night. A young woman was murdered because she had declined a young man's prom invitation. No earthly remedy can heal the effects of such unthinkable acts.

These events scream for resolution from heaven's surplus. The church is God's vessel to carry His supply. Instead of complaining about a lack of security or funding, or the violent nature of video games and other media, we can draw from heaven's surplus of understanding and restoration. When needs arise, we can respond by asking, "What can we bring from heaven to earth to answer these needs?"

The surplus is already *in us*. When the young lady in our church's town was murdered, our family life pastor contacted the school and said that local clergy would make themselves available to counsel grieving students.

The evening of the tragedy, we went to the school gym, but none of the kids showed up. It was prom night; they did not want to be with a bunch of adults and media people. Instead, a couple hundred youths went to the beach in their prom outfits and held a memorial for the slain student. They chose to gather out of the glare of publicity. We went just to be present. You cannot fill a deficit without being present. Some of the pastors wore clerical collars. A teacher asked one of them, "Are you a priest or something? Will you pray or say a few words?"

He said, "Sure." The kids were moved by his words, and he was invited to do the memorial service for the murdered girl. Thousands of young people gathered for that event. Our church saw a need and an opportunity to supply hope, so we rented a couple of movie theaters and invited the youth to see *Heaven Is for Real*, a testimony about heaven that would give them an understanding of life after death.

The response was overwhelming. Even before the official announcement was made, all the tickets were gone. We rented three more theaters to accommodate the families, the school, and the staff. We were not trying to grow our church or to make a name for ourselves. We saw a need, and we filled it. Our pastor didn't need another project. His personal and professional responsibilities were great. His own family was grieving his mother-in-law's death following a battle with cancer. Ministering to a grief-stricken community stretched his soul. But God had already given him a surplus of comfort and peace. It touched his life and overflowed to a hurting community.

Jesus came to overflow *you* so that you could meet needs in the culture all around you. You are an ambassador of surplus. The world's deficit is your invitation to release heaven's supply.

Abundance for God's House

Living from surplus is a spiritual disposition that can be witnessed in the natural realm. When God denied King David his dream of building His temple, the king's longing to bless God was not quelled. David supported his son Solomon's call as temple builder and told him: *"Indeed I have taken much trouble to prepare for the house of the LORD one hundred thousand talents of gold and one million talents of silver, and bronze and iron beyond measure, for it is so abundant. I have prepared timber and stone also, and you may add to them. Moreover there are workmen with you in abundance: woodsmen and stonecutters, and all types of skillful men for every kind of work. Of gold and silver and bronze and iron there is no limit. Arise and begin working, and the LORD be with you"* (1 Chronicles 22:14–16 NKJV). David's "donation" was almost incalculable. He freely received and freely gave from heaven's endless supply!

Invisible Supply

In chapter 1, we talked about what is real but invisible, including thoughts, faith, and God.

The Son is the image of the invisible God, the firstborn over all creation. For in him all things were created: things in heaven and on

earth, visible and invisible, whether thrones or powers or rulers or
authorities; all things have been created through him and for him.

(Colossians 1:15–16)

Let's follow this passage to its logical and biblical conclusion: All
things were created *in Christ*. Additionally, those of us who receive Christ
Jesus as Savior and Lord are *in Him*. (See, for example, Colossians 2:6.)
But He is also *in us*. (See, for example, Ephesians 3:17.) So, what is in us?
Everything.

In Colossians 2, Paul wrote about spiritual maturity. It is not
about looking or acting older. Wrinkles might reveal advancing age,
but they say nothing about maturity. Being spiritually mature means
accessing everything Christ has given. *"For in Christ all the fullness of the
Deity lives in bodily form, and in Christ you have been brought to fullness"*
(Colossians 2:9–10). This is God's surplus, waiting to be revealed in
and through us—individually and corporately! Notice how God sup-
plied the church:

> *Christ himself gave the apostles, the prophets, the evangelists, the pas-*
> *tors and teachers, to equip his people for works of service, so that the*
> *body of Christ may be built up until we all reach unity in the faith*
> *and in the knowledge of the Son of God and become mature, attain-*
> *ing to the whole measure of the fullness of Christ.*
>
> (Ephesians 4:11–13)

God gives ministry gifts to help us live from heaven's surplus. Fullness
is God's desired condition for the church. Many of us are begging God to
bring revival, when He wants to bring *fullness*. Full is the new *new*. We are
to access what we already have until we come to the whole measure of the
fullness of Christ. We are being drawn in by our needs so He can show us
all that He has already prepared for us.

You are not empty but full. You are not living from deficit; you are *in*
surplus. Now, live *from* it.

> ## Who Is in Whom?
>
> Colossians 1:27 says that Christ in you is *"the hope of glory."* Colossians 3:3 says that *"you died, and your life is now hidden with Christ in God."* So, is Christ in you, or are you in Him? The answer is "Yes." Heavenly thinking is paradoxical. But, more than paradox, it is fullness. To say that Christ is in you *and* that you are in Him is not either-or but both. You don't come to Him *for* the answer; you come *with* the answer. Therefore, you can say, "Thank You, Lord! Your divine power has given me everything I need to live a godly life!" (See 2 Peter 1:3.)

Plenty for Everyone

Jesus demonstrated heaven's surplus when He fed the five thousand.[2] The massive crowd came to hear Jesus preach, but there were no dining rooms, delicatessens, or hot dog stands in the area. The people were hungry and away from home. The disciples were hungry, too, and they suggested that Jesus send the people away so they could go and feed themselves.

Jesus' answer was stunning. "No," He said. "You feed them."

Jesus wasn't as concerned with filling people's stomachs as He was with revealing heaven's supply. He put His disciples in a situation that was over their heads. They had their own needs, and they lacked the material means to meet the needs of the crowd. Yet they were about to see what God had already provided—and how willing He was to pour it out.

Jesus drew the disciples into revelation as He often would—with a question, this time to Philip:

> *"Where shall we buy bread for these people to eat?" He asked this only to test him, for he already had in mind what he was going to do. Philip answered him, "It would take more than half a year's wages to buy enough bread for each one to have a bite!"* (John 6:5–7)

Then Andrew said, *"Here is a boy with five small barley loaves and two small fish, but how far will they go among so many?"* (John 6:9).

Jesus brought His men to the end of their natural ideas. They were primed for a miracle. But notice this nuance in the lesson: Giving is essential to receiving, but giving was not the whole story with the loaves and the fish. The boy's mother had packed his lunch and given it to him. But did it multiply in that transaction? No. And when the boy gave his lunch to Andrew, did the number of loaves and fish increase? Not at all.

Even when Andrew gave the food to Jesus, the quantity remained the same: five loaves and two fish. Now watch what Jesus did: *"Taking the five loaves and the two fish and looking up to heaven, he gave thanks and broke the loaves"* (Matthew 14:19). Jesus lifted up the small amount—all they had—to heaven. *He changed its location* and placed it in a dimension not of quantity but of infinite supply.

When Jesus had finished giving thanks and lowered the food, was it enough to feed the crowd? No. It was *more than enough.* Some people focus on the numeric symbolism of the twelve basketfuls that were left over. Not me. I see a God who's not counting, a God who doesn't know when enough is enough.

I believe we are living in a time when goods and commodities that once seemed scarce will become abundant. The scarcity is not because these items are unavailable. It is because they are inaccessible.

Just two or three decades ago, miracles of healing were thought to be rare occurrences, even in church meetings. Now you can watch a miracle a day on YouTube. It's not that miracles were unavailable; they were just harder to access.

The perception of scarcity is not only a spiritual phenomenon. It also applies to the realm of natural resources. For example, about 71 percent of the earth is covered by water,[3] yet nearly one person in nine lacks access to safe drinking water. There is plenty of water, but safe drinking water (from pipes, standpipes, protected dug wells, protected springs, and so forth) is inaccessible to more than 780 million people.[4]

One idea from heaven could change that!

Such ideas have already changed history. In the mid-1800s, Napoleon's important dinner guests used place settings made of gold. Yet only the *most* special guests used cutlery in a metal so rare that bars of it were displayed with the French crown jewels.[5] The metal was *aluminum*, the third most plentiful element in the earth's crust. Anyone wealthy enough to buy a can of Coke has handled a significant amount of the once cost-prohibitive material. Aluminum is no more plentiful today than it was in Napoleon's time. However, it is more accessible—because someone learned to think differently.

Charles Martin Hall was the son of missionaries who left the mission field when they ran out of funding. Physically weakened by ten years of missionary work, and grieving the loss of one of his sons to tropical disease, his father, Heman Hall, became a pastor in Ohio.[6]

Heman's son Charles enrolled in chemistry courses at Oberlin College. Charles's love for chemistry was matched only by his passion for music.[7] He often fell asleep reading chemistry books and awakened early to play from his mother's collection of hymns and classical music. One day, his professor displayed a small piece of shiny metal—it was aluminum. He told the class that the person who made aluminum abundant would change the world and become very rich. Charles told one of his classmates, "I'll be that man."[8]

Each night, Charles experimented in the woodshed behind his parents' house. When he found himself stuck, he played the piano. One night, his sister Julia heard him playing. Instead of joining him, she stayed in bed and listened. The next morning, Julia sparked a breakfast conversation that produced a startling revelation.

"Good morning, Charlie, why were you up so late? It must have been past midnight when I heard you at the piano."

"You know, sis, I've got a new idea for making aluminum."[9]

The answer to Charles's scientific "blockage" had eluded him in the woodshed but became apparent as he played hymns and other music in the midnight hour. It was no small discovery. Charles Martin Hall went on to patent the process of electrolysis that made aluminum accessible to the world. He also founded a company called The Aluminum Company of America, or ALCOA. He left a large portion of his massive estate to fund missions and education throughout Asia.[10] The man whose parents had left the mission field due to scarcity found abundance and became a benefactor to the world!

"In [Christ] *all things consist"* (Colossians 1:17 NKJV). That includes aluminum and water and everything else that we need in order to live on the earth. We are in Christ, and He is in us. The church is *"His body, the fullness of Him who fills all in all"* (Ephesians 1:23 NKJV).

There is plenty for everyone who will receive.

Words Release Supply

It is not your works that will release what God has placed inside you. You have already seen how praise and worship open human eyes to the unseen realm. Words are important in other ways, too. The right words reach into heaven and release its supply.

God told Moses to speak to a rock, and water would come out of it to quench the Israelites' physical thirst. Unfortunately, instead of speaking to the rock, Moses struck it in anger. Nevertheless, God was faithful to supply the water. If Moses had obeyed, not only would the water have been provided, but Moses might also have entered the Promised Land. (See Numbers 20:2–12.) Later, God told the Israelites to shout, and Jericho's walls came down. (See Joshua 6:1–20.) David told Goliath, *"This day the LORD will deliver you into my hands, and I'll strike you down and cut off your head"* (1 Samuel 17:46), and it came to pass. And Jesus declared, *"Truly I tell you, if anyone **says** to this mountain, 'Go, throw yourself into the sea,' and does not doubt in their heart but believes that what they **say** will happen, it will be done for them"* (Mark 11:23).

The wrong words are equally powerful. Repeatedly tell a child that she is stupid, and she will believe it. Wrong words can access the unseen realm of darkness and grant it permission to empower a lie. Think before you speak, and let your words access heaven.

The Real Miracle

Right now, the culture is crying out in deficit, and God is amplifying the message of the finished work of the cross. The deficit that troubles the natural mind is pulling on the full, finished supply already within us. The positional viewpoint we have talked about again and again is this: Thinking *like* heaven means thinking *from* heaven and its surplus. This is how we meet needs.

Miracles manifest in this way, too. We become aware of the fullness of Christ's finished work, and, by faith, we enter into it. Yet the real miracle is what Jesus did two thousand years ago. We are living from its flow to this day! People are receiving salvation as we speak. How does that miracle happen? A person sees who Christ is, receives what Christ did, believes in his heart, and confesses his belief with his mouth. (See Romans 10:8–10.) Whatever day today is, it is the day of salvation! (See 2 Corinthians 6:2.)

Even if you are already saved, there are many heavenly things you haven't yet accessed. Notice that I didn't say you don't have them. I said you have not accessed them. The same is true for me. God has done things that I have yet to partake of. When I do, certain needs will be met in my life and in the lives of others.

You don't have a deficit. You have an *amazing* surplus waiting to be poured out. God will put you in dry places so that He can release rivers of supply through you. He might do it when you think you are too tired to function or to care. When you least expect it, He will give you what the person sitting next to you on an airplane needs...or what the bank teller you are doing business with needs...or what the lady in the back pew of your church needs. His overflow will satisfy their needs and yours.

He is more than enough. *Much more.*

Thinking like Heaven

1. Have you ever misread a situation and acted—or almost acted—on your misunderstanding, as I did with the injured taxi driver? Ask the Father to reveal what really happened in that circumstance and how you might handle future situations differently. What aspect of His answer shakes up your thinking?

2. How well-equipped are you to be God's "waterspout"? Are you basing your evaluation on your supply—or on His? Ask God for His evaluation and then compare/contrast it with your own.

3. Is your weakness (including any weariness, shyness, fears, or past mistakes) an obstacle, or is it an invitation to participate in God's plans? Explain.

4. Name some things that are in you due to the fact that you are in Christ. Which of these things surprise you the most? How does "finding" them change your outlook? Your choices?

5. Imagine yourself in Philip's or Andrew's shoes when Jesus fed the five thousand. How might you have responded to Jesus' questions and instruction? Describe how the finished work of the cross either confirms or challenges your response.

Notes

1. *Biblesoft's New Exhaustive Strong's Numbers and Concordance*, s.v. "poneros" (NT 4190).
2. Accounts of this miracle appear in all four Gospels. See Matthew 14:13–21; Mark 6:30–44; Luke 9:10–17; John 6:1–14.
3. "How much water is there on, in, and above the Earth?", http://water.usgs.gov/edu/earthhowmuch.html.
4. Estimated with data from *Progress on Drinking Water and Sanitation: 2012 Update*, Foreword, 2, Joint Monitoring Programme (JMP) for Water Supply and Sanitation, UNICEF and World Health Organization, http://www.unicef.org/media/files/JMPreport2012.pdf. See also "Improved and Unimproved Water and Sanitation Facilities," WHO/UNICEF Joint Monitoring Programme (JMP) for Water Supply and Sanitation, http://www.wssinfo.org/definitions-methods/watsan-categories/.
5. Sam Kean, "Aluminum: It Used to Be More Precious than Gold," *Blogging the Periodic Table*, http://www.slate.com/articles/health_and_science/elements/features/2010/blogging_the_periodic_table/aluminum_it_used_to_be_more_precious_than_gold.html.
6. Junius Edwards, *The Immortal Woodshed: The Story of the Inventor Who Brought Aluminum to America* (New York: Dodd, Mead & Company, 1955), 5.
7. Ibid., 11–12.
8. Ibid., 37–38.
9. Ibid., 52.
10. Daniel H. Bays and Ellen Widmer, eds., *China's Christian Colleges: Cross-Cultural Connections, 1900–1950* (Stanford, CA: Stanford University Press, 2009), 244–245.

11

Repaired and Restored

 Bob Hazlett @bob_hazlett
When you talk to God, people call that prayer.
When God talks to you, people call you "crazy."
Maybe crazy is talking without expecting an
answer. #ThinklikeHeaven

When I spoke at the New Age church that I mentioned in chapter 1, they asked me to come back and explain "that healing-in-the-name-of-Jesus stuff." They thought it was just another technique for their repertoire. It wasn't, but it was an invitation to bring heaven to earth. So, I accepted.

I prepared a seminar called "Three Dimensions of Divine Healing." I'm not sure what that meant in New Age lingo, but I was referring to spirit, soul, and body. The title caught on, and a couple hundred people showed up. As far as I know, my wife and I were the only two who had a relationship with Jesus. We brought the Word of God and the atmosphere of heaven with us.

About fifteen minutes into my talk, a woman raised her hand. No one had ever asked me a question in church before. I set aside my surprise and asked, "Ma'am, do you have a question?"

"Well," she said, "I have to leave the meeting, but I really need healing."

"Perfect!" I thought her healing would be a great demonstration for a roomful of spiritual seekers. I invited her to the front and asked, "Where is the problem?"

She said, "My left shoulder is frozen in place. The pain is really bad."

I told her, "I am going to pray for you in the name of Jesus. I'm not going to touch you, because healing is not about the energy in my hands. It's about the name of Jesus. He loves you, and He died for you. When I pray in His name, your arm will be completely healed. Are you ready?"

"Yes," she said.

"In the name of Jesus, I command this shoulder to be healed. Every muscle and nerve be loosed. Shoulder, be completely healed and move, in Jesus' name." Then I said, "Now, ma'am, move your arm."

She said, "I can't."

Lord, I prayed, *this is not a good time for a lesson in how not to heal. Please just heal her.* Then I remembered that Jesus had to pray twice before a certain man's healing was complete.

> *Some people brought a blind man and begged Jesus to touch him. He took the blind man by the hand and led him outside the village. When he had spit on the man's eyes and put his hands on him, Jesus asked, "Do you see anything?" He looked up and said, "I see people; they look like trees walking around." Once more Jesus put his hands on the man's eyes. Then his eyes were opened, his sight was restored, and he saw everything clearly.* (Mark 8:22–25)

If Jesus prayed twice before the man saw clearly, I could pray twice for this woman's shoulder to move. I explained the example to her and then continued, saying, "In the name of Jesus, I command this arm to be healed." I asked her to move her arm.

"I can't."

My inner conversation with God heated up. *Lord, people are watching You and thinking this doesn't work.*

In that moment, the Holy Spirit spoke to me. "It's not a physical ailment. It's spiritual. An arthritic spirit has traced her family line on her mother's side. Her grandmother had arthritis, and so did her mother. Now she is developing it."

I wondered how best to explain what the Holy Spirit had revealed. I decided to share a story. "A woman once came to church crippled like this." I bent over to give her the idea. "Jesus said, 'A negative spiritual influence has impacted her physical body—a spirit of infirmity.'"

Then I explained the situation to the crowd. "I am going to pray, because a negative spiritual influence has attached itself to this woman's genetics. It was passed down through her grandmother and her mother."

Next, I addressed the woman again. "Is that right? Did your mother and grandmother have arthritis?"

Through her tears, she said, "Yes."

That was when God said, "If you are willing to look like a fool for thirty seconds, I'll make you look like a genius."

I had already looked foolish for longer than that. Another thirty seconds would not hurt. I said, "If anybody else in this room has this kind of negative spiritual influence, stand to your feet." Then I prayed.

Boom! The woman's shoulder was unfrozen, and other arthritic people were healed, too!

It was just a matter of speaking to the mountain *until it moved*. I really didn't know what I was doing. I doubt the disciples knew what they were doing back in the day. God asks only that we do what we know to do so He can repair the broken things in people's lives.

World Repair

The Hebrew phrase *tikkun olam* means "world repair." The phrase originated in classic rabbinic literature and was recited three times daily by Jews in the *Aleinu* prayer.[1] The idea of repairing the world is God's idea, and He calls us to be involved.

God Can Use Anyone

Whatever has been broken due to the fall of man, God will repair and restore—and He will use you in the process. Don't rely too heavily on your areas of expertise. God is not looking for experts. He is looking for people who are willing to follow His direction.

That is how I got involved with a "pharmaceutical mission." A woman at one of my meetings was healed of severe ADHD and another less severe challenge. She had been taking prescribed medications for about ten years. Once she was healed, she was able to quit taking them.

When I returned to her city the following year, she brought her husband to the meeting. He worked in the pharmaceutical industry, so his wife's healing had gotten his attention. But he was also skeptical. "I know this is God," he said, "but I don't understand all this healing and prophecy stuff. Could you just pray for me?"

"Sure," I said. All I knew about him was his line of work, but as I prayed, I saw pictures of him. "I see you working on a project involving the blood, but God is going to switch you to a project having to do with the brain. I see God using you to develop natural ways of healing brain issues like Alzheimer's, Parkinson's, and other neurological problems, but you will not need to use human stem cells."

Then I saw a process and shared it with him. "I see you in the lab. God is going to accelerate the approval process for your work. It would normally take three years, but I see you standing before a group of people in a year's time."

As I described what would happen, he interrupted me. "You have to stop there. That's classified information."

Seriously? I thought. *How cool is that?*

Twelve minutes later, I finished praying. A month after that, I received an e-mail with an MP3 file of the prophecy. He wrote, "Listen to what you said, and I'll tell you what happened after that."

It was amazing to see how God had allowed someone with a bachelor's degree to speak to a Ph.D. and sound intelligent. My last science class was in high school. I was not equipped to discuss chemistry at the level of pharmaceuticals. But God was.

The man explained that at the time I prayed for him, he had been working on a diabetes project. Two weeks later, his supervisor reassigned him to an Alzheimer's project. Then he got an idea about how to extract cells without using embryonic stem cells. He presented it to his supervisor, who was impressed with the plan. One by one, the chain of command approved the process, and within a month's time, a year's work was accomplished.

That's how creative God is! The scientist and I were both blown away by what God was doing. He asked me to pray and see if God would reveal anything else about his research.

Before I fell asleep that night, I told God, "Lord, I don't know what to tell this guy, but if You have something in mind, I'm listening."

God gave me a hilarious dream in which someone held out both hands and said, "This is a fat molecule, and this is a protein molecule." Then the person began to dance and sing a peculiar song: "Fat is beautiful, fat is beautiful, fat is beautiful. The beauty is in the fat."

I thought, *God, You have a sense of humor! But no way am I going to sing this song to a Ph.D.*

Instead, I told the man, "I feel like God is saying you will find something in fat molecules that will bring a breakthrough to your research."

For three months, I heard nothing. I thought, *I'm the worst scientific prophecy guy in the world! What was I thinking?*

Then I got a very exciting e-mail. "You won't believe this," wrote the scientist. "I just got back from a stem cell research conference in which the deep fat tissues in human gums were described as the greatest potential source of stem cells!"

I didn't know there was fat in my gums. But God did.

My friend was not the first scientist to discover that God can speak to him. As an agricultural chemist, George Washington Carver discovered hundreds of uses for peanuts, soybeans, pecans, and sweet potatoes. Among the innovative ideas to improve the prospects of Southern farmers were his recipes and advancements in regard to adhesives, axle grease, bleach, buttermilk, chili sauce, instant coffee, mayonnaise, meat tenderizer, fuel briquettes, ink, linoleum, metal polish, paper, plastic, pavement, shaving cream, talcum powder, shoe polish, synthetic rubber, and wood stain.[2]

The conviction Carver lived by was also the research method by which he worked:

> God is going to reveal things to us He never revealed before if we put our hands in His. No books ever go into my laboratory. The thing I am to do and the way of doing it are revealed to me. I never have to grope for methods. The method is revealed to me the moment I am inspired to create something new. Without God to draw aside the curtain, I would be helpless.[3]

God really wants to use us to do His will!

The God of the Now

Miracles don't happen only at the time when we see them manifest. They happen when we become aware of what God has already done and access it by faith. God doesn't live in the past or the future. He is always in the now. Notice what He said through the prophet Isaiah:

> *In the time of my favor I will answer you, and in the day of salvation*
> *I will help you; I will keep you and will make you to be a covenant for*
> *the people, to restore the land and to reassign its desolate inheritances,*

to say to the captives, "Come out," and to those in darkness, "Be free!"
(Isaiah 49:8–9)

God's promise has not expired. It applies *now*. Today is the day of salvation, and not just for people. The passage from Isaiah reveals three areas that God promises to repair and restore:

1. God will restore the land.

2. God will reassign desolate inheritances.

3. God will speak freedom to captives.

In fact, God used Moses to fulfill all three areas on behalf of the Israelites. He told Moses He would lead the people into a land flowing with milk and honey—and He did. He also promised to give to the Israelites cities they had not built and wells they had not dug. As captives, they had no cities or buildings of their own, even though, centuries earlier, God had promised Abraham that his descendants would have their own land. Now their desolate inheritances were reassigned. And, through Moses, God told the captives, "Come out!"

Repair and restoration are *now*. *"In the time of my favor I will answer you, and in the day of salvation I will help you"* (Isaiah 49:8). In 2 Corinthians 6:2, after referring to this promise from Isaiah, Paul wrote, *"I tell you, now is the time of God's favor, now is the day of salvation."* These promises are in the now for everyone who will perceive them and receive them by faith.

Are you wondering what happened to *your* now? Stay in tune with the promise. Don't just live toward it—*live from it*. Act like you already have it, even when you don't see proof that it is real. Breakthrough doesn't come when you *get* the job, the spouse, or the financial means you have been praying to receive. Breakthrough happens the moment you *believe*.

God can use others to help you break through. But only Christ within you can empower you to live your breakthrough and to become a breakthrough for someone else. Christ in you is the hope of glory. But when Christ flows out of you, His glory is manifested *now*.

Lost Promises Fulfilled

A desolate inheritance is a promise that was never claimed, assigned, or accessed. Promises of well-being, of fruitfulness, and of peace belong to people and even to nations. When you meet a gang leader, for example, ask God to reveal the desolate inheritance that awaits fulfillment. The person may be called to leadership in ministry but is using his or her gifts in ways that are more culturally familiar. That leader is *"God's handiwork, created in Christ Jesus to do good works, which God prepared in advance for* [him or her] *to do"* (Ephesians 2:10). The promise has not expired. Today is the day of salvation.

His Glory in the Now

I believe that, sometimes, we are too passive. We are waiting for God to do the impossible, but He is waiting for us to act upon what is possible for us to do. God loves to put His *super* on our natural!

We are waiting for His glory to cover the earth as the waters cover the sea. (See Habakkuk 2:14.) It will happen, but I doubt that a great mist will roll out of heaven and blanket us. We get caught up in mystical ideas. His glory *can* be mystical, but it is also manifested in ordinary ways. When you pray for a gang leader, or when you speak life to a stranger in a hotel lobby, you are releasing Christ into the situation. He is manifested when you give a little extra tip to someone who provides a service for you, or when you show mercy to the unkind. I believe His glory covers the earth when you and I recognize and access Christ within us and release the hope of glory for others to receive. That is when this planet tastes heaven!

You have probably heard prophetic words about the last-day generation and the great move of God coming to those, for example, between the ages of eighteen and thirty-five. I liked hearing those prophecies until I turned thirty-six. Then I was excited to hear that the Lord would use people who were in their forties. Now, prophecies about people in their fifties sound good. So, who is this nameless and faceless generation we talk about? And who decided the age range? God is using eighty- and ninety-year-olds as we speak.

The generation God is interested in is the one that seeks His face. His glory is always in the *now*. The time of miracles becoming commonplace is already here. We are not waiting for God to move. God is waiting for us to let Him move. This is our time, and today is our day. Jesus did it all on the cross, and He wants us to access *all of it* by faith. The moment we believe that the people we pray for are healed, the breakthrough comes, and God's glory is seen—even when the results don't appear evident.

We think real faith is seen when mountains move. God honors faith that prays and that speaks to the mountain, even when it doesn't seem to move at all. Remember that Moses accomplished his mission, but it took forty years. In fact, Moses did not live to see the people physically enter the Promised Land. When God met Moses at the burning bush, He explained that *I Am* was sending him as a deliverer. (See Exodus 3:7–15.) In other words, "I am in the now. You won't find Me in the slavery mind-set of Israel's past or in some future date when you think the grass will be greener. I Am, Moses. I just *am*."

Jesus didn't say how many times you should speak to the mountain. He said simply to speak to it. (See, for example, Mark 11:23–24.) It is impossible to speak God's Word and get no results. When the mountain appears not to move, you can rest assured that something *is* moving: *your faith*.

The mountain moves, as long as you don't quit. If you don't see it move the first time you pray about it and speak to it, then pray and speak to it again. Today is the day of salvation. God's glory is seen in the now.

David and the Ark

The worshipper King David brought the ark of the covenant—God's dwelling place on earth—to Jerusalem. (See 1 Chronicles 15:1–3, 25.) In bringing it to Jerusalem, David brought heaven to earth and refocused the culture on

God's glory. It was a joyous occasion. *"All Israel brought up the ark of the covenant of the LORD with shouts, with the sounding of rams' horns and trumpets, and of cymbals, and the playing of lyres and harps. As the ark of the covenant of the LORD was entering the City of David, Michal daughter of Saul watched from a window. And when she saw King David dancing and celebrating, she despised him in her heart"* (1 Chronicles 15:28–29; see also 2 Samuel 6:16–22). Yet David cared little about looking foolish or being ridiculed. He loved God with abandon, cherished His presence, and longed to see His glory manifested in the midst of the people.

Orders to Go

Several years ago, I had a dream in which I walked into a restaurant, stepped up to the counter, and said, "I want my order to go."

The person at the register pointed at a small pub table off to the side and said, "Go wait over there."

A father and son were sitting at the table. As I sat beside the son, he said, "You need to understand Matthew chapter thirteen. It's about the kingdom."

I awoke from the dream and asked God, "Is this dream from You?"

He said, "It is, but it isn't just for you. It is for the church. I am about to give the church orders to go. First, they must understand the relationship between Father and Son, and they must understand My kingdom. I am going to release understanding of fatherhood, sonship, daughterhood, and motherhood. Then the kingdom will be released in greater ways. I will teach you about this through Matthew chapter thirteen."

Chapters 12 and 13 of the book of Matthew span a transition in Jesus' ministry. Before Matthew 13, Jesus ministered primarily at synagogues and in houses. Then Matthew 13:1–2 says, *"Jesus went out of the house and sat by the lake. Such large crowds gathered around him that he got into a boat and sat in it, while all the people stood on the shore.*" Jesus stopped ministering in synagogues and quit holding small meetings in people's houses. He had a new platform that reached more people.

Among the people Jesus reached were two types He had faced all along. We saw both of them in the healing of the paralytic man recorded in Matthew 9 and Mark 2. One type is the spiritual skeptic, and the other is the spiritual spectator. Most people with strong ties to the synagogue were spiritual skeptics. The religious leaders folded their arms and scowled at Jesus, saying, in essence, "Who do You think You are? What does the son of a carpenter know about forgiving a man's sin?" They were offended because they had a limited view of who Jesus was.

The friends of the paralyzed man did not ask for Jesus' credentials. They knew He healed the sick, so they brought their friend to Him. The house meeting was so crowded that they had to rip open the roof just to get their friend inside. Although they believed, they were spiritual spectators who sat on the edge of their seats and waited for Jesus to do something. "Come on, Jesus! Raise the dead. Heal the sick. Cleanse the leper. Do it, Jesus! We are watching." They peered in the windows and through cracks in the doors. Jesus never chased them away; He accommodated them.

These two types still exist today. Many people in the church are spiritual skeptics. They are jaded and passive, and they criticize those who expect to see supernatural manifestations of God's kingdom. They want to go to church without *being* the church. Others are spiritual spectators. They are not skeptical—they take a different tack. They love to go to conferences and experience exuberant worship. They travel from place to place to "get more of God," not realizing that He will overflow within them wherever they are. They love seeing miracles, but, like ticketholders at a sporting event, they are satisfied to watch.

There is good news: God is turning skeptics into kingdom believers, and spectators into His kingdom army. He is transitioning the church and sending us beyond the walls of the house. God is empowering us to bring heaven into secular settings and throughout our communities.

Step up to the counter. He is giving you orders to go.

Your Platform Is Ready

Jesus transitioned from ministering in synagogues and houses to ministering from a boat on the water. Almost everything in the local culture revolved around water, including people's businesses. Agriculture wasn't very lucrative, but the fishing industry was. Additionally, Israel was under Roman rule, and the trappings of Roman influence—such as armies, artwork, books, and architectural plans—were imported on ships.

Previously, the only thing that had almost never involved boats was ministry. But when Jesus stepped into a boat, it became His pulpit. It was a platform for God's kingdom from which He released heaven on earth. It looked nothing like a synagogue, and it certainly wasn't a house. But it was effective—*very* effective—for the kingdom.

We don't always recognize the platforms that have been made available to us. Some of them don't resemble the usual venues for ministry, so we discount them. Consequently, not only do we miss prime opportunities to repair our world, but we also miss divine clues to our own destinies. It happens all the time. Often, such oversights are revealed to me when I have a conversation with someone that goes something like the following. The person begins by saying, "I want to live my life for God."

I ask, "Well, what do you want to do?"

"I've thought about becoming a doctor, but I want to do missions work and heal the sick."

"Do you get good grades in school?" I ask. "Do you like to learn? Do you like medicine?"

"Yes, but I want to be in the ministry."

"What if you were on the mission field and the people needed good hygiene or preventive health care? Praying for them is powerful, but sometimes medical knowledge is what they need. What if you could bring supernatural healing *and* the medical insights to help them to live healthy and stay well?"

The pulpit isn't the only platform in the kingdom. Perhaps you are called to the realm of government or law or communications. You might be a makeup artist called to minister to high-powered people behind the scenes. These are potent venues for bringing heaven to earth. Many other "boats" exist in modern society—thousands of them. Take your pick, because kingdom people are needed to pilot every single one! Don't leave the church or forsake the local community of believers. Just "get out of the house," as Jesus did.

Interestingly, Jesus began speaking in parables during His ministry transition. The custom in the synagogues was to read from the scrolls, which Jesus did. (See Luke 4:16–21.) But now, instead of quoting from scrolls, Jesus told parables about investors, judges, farmers, and much more. (See, for example, Matthew 25; Luke 18:1–14; Mark 4:1–34.) These relatable stories allowed Jesus to present the deep things of His kingdom in easy-to-understand language.

So, as Jesus' platform changed, His approach shifted. He came out of the synagogues and houses and released Himself into the broader culture, immersing it in the atmosphere of heaven. We need to follow His example and use every means available to reach people with the culture of the kingdom. If Jesus were incarnated today, I believe He would tweet the gospel, post it on Facebook, and share photos of healed lepers on Instagram. He might even take a selfie with Zacchaeus. The caption would read, "This is My new friend, the tax collector. He's going to pay back everyone he overcharged!"

To *be* the church, we have to venture outside our buildings and speak in ways that society can hear and understand. And we need to be patient with people who lack a frame of reference for the things we say. When Jesus' disciples asked why He spoke in parables, He explained that the people were unable to understand the kingdom because their hearts were hardened. (See Matthew 13:10–15.)

Then He told the disciples, "*But blessed are your eyes because they see, and your ears because they hear*" (Matthew 13:16). This is hilarious, because even the disciples had trouble "hearing." But Jesus used His platforms well; He patiently trained His inner circle both to hear the truth and to share it. After His ascension, His disciples used their platforms well, too. They changed the world.

Now it is our turn.

Identity Test and Transition

There is another aspect of Jesus' ministry transition that speaks to us today. It is revealed in a visit recorded in Matthew's gospel.

While Jesus was still talking to the crowd, his mother and brothers stood outside, wanting to speak to him. Someone told Him, "Your mother and brothers are standing outside, wanting to speak to you."

(Matthew 12:46–47)

It was immediately after this unexpected visit that Jesus went outside the house and taught the people from the boat. I believe the visit from Jesus' family members was a pivotal test of His identity. His mother, Mary, knew that He was the Son of God, but His siblings were not so sure. They had already questioned Jesus' identity and wondered about His sanity. *"They [once] went to take charge of him, for they said, 'He is out of his mind'"* (Mark 3:21).

The backstory of the visit recorded in Matthew 12 is uncertain, but it may have been initiated by Mary. Perhaps she just wanted to see her boy. Or maybe family business needed tending to. We know Mary was widowed, and we know Jesus was her oldest son. In their culture, He would have been expected to take over the family business and to serve as the head of the home.

Jesus knew that cultural traditions were incompatible with His mission. If He hadn't known who He was, He could have done many good things but missed the "God things" He was destined to do. So, His identity was tested when His family came calling. Notice how Jesus responded.

He replied to [the person who had informed Him of His family's presence], *"Who is my mother, and who are my brothers?" Pointing to his disciples, he said, "Here are my mother and my brothers. For whoever does the will of my Father in heaven is my brother and sister and mother."*

(Matthew 12:48–50)

For Jesus, there was no turning back from His mission or His larger, spiritual family. His identity and purpose were crystal clear. He redefined Himself, not by disrespecting His loved ones but by appropriately honoring

His heavenly Father and His heavenly identity. When His family came to visit, He held His sonship above His earthly identifiers, and His ministry transitioned *that very day*.

Our world is changing. The church is in transition. Individually and corporately, our identities are being tested, spiritually and otherwise. Some people enter the shift knowing who they are. They affirm the fullness of their identity, even when friends and loved ones prefer to view them narrowly. Skeptics may tell them, "I remember you from back in the day. You were an average student. How can you run a large firm?" Yet, they respond confidently, "You're right. My grades were so-so. But there is a lot about me that you don't know. I know who I am, and I understand what I was created to do."

Other people are not so self-assured, and many of them miss their transitions. They say, "You're right. I was an average student. Running a company is probably over my head. I'd better play it safe."

Transitions are necessary to growth. Remember that these transitions don't happen when you step forward; they happen when you believe. The leaving doesn't take us into something new. Believing who we are takes us there. We are children of God, supernatural beings, new creatures in Christ. New seasons await us. The moment we receive them, the transition is accomplished.

Flip the Conversation

Do you leave your house with a to-do list as long as your arm and then swing by the drive-thru coffeehouse to refuel? Java on the run is an American staple of which Swedes might disapprove. To them, "coffee is an experience."[4] They call it *fika*, a word that flips the letters of *kaffi*, their word for coffee. *Fika* is both noun and verb. The noun "refers to the combination of coffee and usually some sort of sweet snack. But fika, as a verb, is the act of partaking in a Swedish social institution."[5] For Swedes, drinking coffee is relational.

Repair and restoration are relational, too. And both can happen over a cup of coffee. When we discussed the supernatural power of love, we studied Jesus' conversation with a Samaritan woman who came to draw water from a well. Jesus flipped His request for a drink into a release of spiritual refreshment. A simple conversation for two led to a healing and revival service for many. (See John 4:1–42.)

Similar opportunities present themselves every day. Seemingly chance encounters can release God's repair and restoration like a flood! We just need to become aware of them and be willing to interrupt our to-do lists. We can take three simple cues from what Jesus did in His encounter with the woman at the well.

1. Jesus stopped at the well to rest, but He did not equate His weariness with weakness. In moments of personal need or physical weakness, we often believe we are unable to help others. The opposite is true. God's strength is perfected in our weakness. (See 2 Corinthians 12:9.) Jesus was refreshed as He refreshed the Samaritan woman. When the disciples returned, they were baffled by His vigor.

> *His disciples urged him, "Rabbi, eat something." But he said to them, "I have food to eat that you know nothing about." Then his disciples said to each other, "Could someone have brought him food?" "My food," said Jesus, "is to do the will of him who sent me and to finish his work."*
>
> (John 4:31–34)

2. Jesus understood that God's heavenly resources were greater than His earthly ones. The disciples left Him at the well so they could go find provisions. Jesus had no canteen and no access to an ATM machine. Yet He turned His lack of resources into a citywide revival!

3. Jesus told the woman what God had already been saying to her. Her life was storied in the town where she lived. People saw her as a fading flower, wilted by hard living. But God knew that a spiritual drink would make her bloom again. She did bloom, and she shared the fragrance of new life with others.

Bringing heaven to earth should not leave you tired and parched. It should revitalize and refresh you! You won't be more effective by trying harder. Just be yourself—and *fika*. Sit down with your cup and fill the cups of others. Flip everyday conversations, and your platform will follow you wherever you go.

What Repair and Restoration Look Like

Do you know about the "little lady who made a big war"? Some have quoted Abraham Lincoln as coining the phrase to describe Harriet Beecher Stowe. She did not physically start a war, but her book *Uncle Tom's Cabin* rocked America's thinking on slavery.

I can barely imagine a more demonic idea than buying, selling, and owning human beings, especially knowing that Christ paid with His life to set captives free. The diseased thinking behind slavery had infected our culture and our world. But heaven had the antidote. Once mind-sets changed, slavery would end. So God reached into Harriet Beecher Stowe's heart and used her to spark a shift.

The process began in church. That is not surprising, since Stowe's father, several of her siblings, and her husband were all preachers.[6]

> Suddenly, like the unrolling of a picture, the scene of the death of Uncle Tom passed before her mind. So strongly was she affected that it was with difficulty she could keep from weeping aloud. Immediately on returning home she took pen and paper and wrote out the vision which had been, as it were, blown into her mind as by the rushing of a mighty wind.[7]

Stowe had wanted to be a preacher, but the culture said women could not preach. God was undeterred. He gave Stowe a vision that unleashed her voice and snapped cultural norms. Her book prompted changes in America's laws and economic structure. Imagine: A woman taught to be quiet in church got so far out of her mind and into God's mind that she spoke to millions, and is still speaking!

Slavery as an institution was abolished in the nineteenth century, but the world's problems are not over (and slavery continues to exist in various forms, as well). We can easily feel overwhelmed by the many issues we face. But worry and fear help no one. Repair and restoration don't spring from anxiety—they flow from hope. People who see the unseen can bring heaven to earth. Peaceful warriors, like Harriet Beecher Stowe, who are willing to become vulnerable and to swim against cultural currents are poised to release God's ways in the earth. They are not afraid of naysayers or the discomforts of change. They are willing to live in the fray for His glory.

Cultural deficiencies like slavery can be healed without bloodshed. If we release the kingdom's brand of "violence"—the rushing, irresistible force of God's love and truth—He will repair our world and transform our culture without vitriol, hatred, and societal rifts. All it takes is one soul who is willing to press against *what is* and toward *what can be*.

> Twenty-five years [after her book's initial impact] Mrs. Stowe wrote a letter to one of her children, of this period of her life: "I well remember the winter you were a baby and I was writing *Uncle Tom's Cabin*. My heart was bursting with the anguish excited by the cruelty and injustice our nation was showing to the slave, and praying God to let me do a little, and to cause my cry to be heard. I remember many a night weeping over you as you lay sleeping beside me, and I thought of the slave mothers whose babes were torn from them."[8]

Stories like Harriet Beecher Stowe's remind us of the power of God-given identity and destiny. They urge us to race toward God and plead, "Lord, cause me to dwell on thoughts of righteousness to such a degree that the thinking of unrighteous people would be changed. Help me to understand Your authority so fully that when I face situations that oppose Your kingdom, I can continue to think like heaven and to help others see that Your kingdom is here."

Today, I believe God is raising up men and women like Harriet Beecher Stowe. The devil wants us to be at war with one another, but God's kingdom comes with peace. My hope tells me that life will be valued again, from conception to the grave. Marriage will be honored as the joining of a man and a woman. God's design for the family will be restored, even where it has been systematically devalued. I believe these things will happen because God has done them before. Who can stop Him from doing them again? And whom will He use but us?

A book changed the mind-set of nineteenth-century America. It moved a president's heart and affected millions more. Harriet Beecher

Stowe believed that God was the author of *Uncle Tom's Cabin* and that she was His instrument.

We are His instruments, too.

A Final Word

Those who think like heaven are carriers of heaven. *You* are a carrier of heaven. Your assignment might be less public than Harriet Beecher Stowe's—or of broader consequence than Abraham Lincoln's. Whether you are behind the scenes or in front of millions, the presence of God in you is waiting to be released into the culture, transforming the people around you. When it does, even people you have never met will become carriers, too.

In your person, you bear Christ, the hope of glory. Nothing is more powerful than His presence. Whatever mountain stands before you is reduced to dust before the One who lives inside you. So, keep your eyes on Him. Continue peering into the unseen. Listen to what He is saying, and shout it from every platform He provides. Allow Him to shape your perspective and to use you in unlikely ways and in unexpected moments.

Isaiah prophesied Christ as the *"Repairer of Broken Walls, Restorer of Streets with Dwellings"* (Isaiah 58:12). Christ came, finished His work, and commissioned us to become repairers of broken walls and restorers of streets with dwellings. Jesus said, *"He who believes in Me, the works that I do he will do also; and greater works than these he will do, because I go to My Father"* (John 14:12 NKJV).

We are here to repair and to restore in His name! What greater works could there be? Yet it is so simple that a child can do it. The kingdom of God is received by God's kids. You don't need a Ph.D. or a ministerial certificate. Those things are good, but they are not the answer. God wants to restore lands, reassign desolate inheritances, and speak freedom to captives. He can do these things through a conversation over coffee, by a "chance" meeting in an airport, or in the midst of a city grieved by murder. All it takes is one person who thinks like heaven and is willing to do and to say what the Father is doing and saying.

It is just that simple. *And you are just that person.* "[God] walks everywhere incognito,"[9] as C. S. Lewis wrote, because He is in you. My prayer is that, through your life, lost people and lost things…cultural deficits…minds and hearts…and even nations would be made new as you think like heaven.

Thinking like Heaven

1. Thirty seconds is a long time when you think you look foolish. When was the last time that doing the right thing made you feel that way? How did you respond? Ask God to show you something about the situation that you did not know before.

2. Are you still waiting for a breakthrough that seems out of reach? Is it really? How might your perceptions be misleading you?

3. Ask God what your "orders to go" look like. How does He want to use you to turn skeptics into kingdom believers and spectators into His kingdom army? Are any vestiges of these two types (skeptic and spectator) still operating in your life?

4. What are your God-given platforms? How are they different from one another? How are they similar? What is your perfect platform? How does your identity determine your platforms? Ask God to fine-tune your understanding of the platforms He has given you.

5. Here is your *fika* assignment: Meet someone on his or her own turf. Care about what the other person cares about. Show it by finding a topic of conversation that is relevant to him or her. Then listen for an opportunity to "flip" the conversation—to transition to a spiritual topic. After you do this, ask yourself the following questions: Was it hard? Rewarding? What might God say about it?

Notes

1. Rabbi Paul Steinberg, "Where does the concept of tikkun olam (repairing the world) originate, and is it a mitzvah (commandment) or does it hold the same level of importance as a mitzvah?", Jewish Values Online, http://www.jewishvaluesonline.org/594 [click on "Conservative Answer by Rabbi Paul Steinberg"].
2. William J. Federer, *George Washington Carver: His Life & Faith in His Own Words* (St. Louis, MO: Amerisearch, Inc., 2002), 15, 17–18.
3. Ibid., 53.
4. Yael Averbuch, "In Sweden, the Fika Experience," *New York Times*, November 12, 2013, http://www.nytimes.com/2013/11/13/sports/soccer/in-sweden-the-fika-experience.html?_r=0.
5. Ibid.
6. John Deedy, "A Little Lady Who Made a Big War," *New York Times*, November 7, 1976, Travel Section, 21, see http://select.nytimes.com/mem/archive/pdf?res=F10617FB355D1B758DDDAE0894D9415B868BF1D3.
7. Eric J. Sundquist, ed., *New Essays on Uncle Tom's Cabin* [The American Novel series] (New York: Cambridge University Press, 1986), 8.
8. William Lyon Phelps, *Howells, James, Bryant and Other Essays* (New York: The Macmillan Company, 1924), 186, http://utc.iath.virginia.edu/articles/n2eswlpat.html.
9. C. S. Lewis, *Letters to Malcolm: Chiefly on Prayer* (Orlando, FL: Harcourt, 2002), 75.

About the Author

Bob Hazlett is a sought-after speaker, author, and mentor. He travels extensively throughout the United States and internationally, with strong healing and prophetic gifts accompanying his ministry. Bob is a friend to leaders, having a passion to empower people in spiritual gifts so that they may fulfill their life purpose. He is the founder of Touch of Fire Ministries, which encourages leaders and enables individuals to live prophetically and to walk powerfully. He also developed "Future University," an online prophetic training school at www.bobhazlett.org. Bob lives in Connecticut with his wife, Kimberly, and their two daughters, April and Abby.

For more information about Bob Hazlett or for additional resources, visit www.bobhazlett.org or contact info@bobhazlett.org.

Welcome to Our House!

We Have a Special Gift for You

It is our privilege and pleasure to share in your love of Christian books. We are committed to bringing you authors and books that feed, challenge, and enrich your faith.

To show our appreciation, we invite you to sign up to receive a specially selected **Reader Appreciation Gift**, with our compliments. Just go to the Web address at the bottom of this page.

God bless you as you seek a deeper walk with Him!

WE HAVE A GIFT FOR YOU. VISIT:

whpub.me/nonfictionthx

WHITAKER
HOUSE